Growing Up Riparian

A COLUMBIA RIVER BOYHOOD

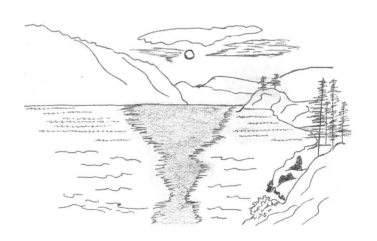

T. M. Johnson

Every boy needs a river running through his youth. This was mine.

T. M. Johnson

ISBN: 1461198666
ISBN-13: 9781461198666

When I was younger, I could remember everything —
whether it happened or not.

Mark Twain

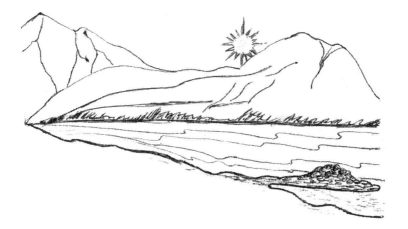

For Dad: In gratitude for bringing us to the river

For Marika: If it wasn't quite this way, it should have been

FORWARD

Truth and memory. Truth in memory. As I pair these two words and think about what I have written here, I would like to maintain that memory is the recollection of the truth, of events, experiences—emotional and physical—people and places true. I would like to think the phrase "I remember…" invokes and reveals a bygone truth, stark and real. But I found it does not work that way. I suspect memory, though unintentionally, may sometimes be hearsay masquerading as truth.

Though most memories of those days on the river I recalled with photographic clarity, others returned as fragments. In some cases I was able to assist memory by returning to the former haunts and playgrounds of my youth. For the others I relied on family and friends to smooth the burrs of hazy recollection. Then interesting things happened. In some cases my consultants repaired the fragment, made it whole. Others, to my confusion, replayed the memory with a spin of their own. Some stated flat out they did not remember the experience or incident at all. In those cases I feared I was the victim of a hyperactive imagination. I knew to validate my memories—lest they become fiction—I needed to abide by what I believed to be the factual past. In those moments of doubt I could only rely on faith and write what truth seemed to fit. Therefore I can only say I told the truth as I remembered it.

As Twain's Huckleberry Finn said of the book *The Adventures of Tom Sawyer*, "There was things which he stretched, but mainly he told the truth." And, stretchers aside, in what follows, mainly so have I.

Growing up Riparian

(**Ri-par-ian**: relating to or located on the bank of a
natural watercourse [as a river])

PROLOGUE

It was on the cusp of two seasons when our family made the
move upriver to the Crane ranch. When Francis G. Crane, one of
Dad's flight students offered him a job as foreman of his apple ranch
that August of 1953, Dad gave up his job with Wenatchee Air Service. (The move brought an end to his fledgling career in aviation;
Dad never piloted another plane). Francis Crane sent a large farm
truck and a few ranch hands to move the household items and furni-
ture from our Wenatchee home to the two-story house on the river.
This rambling ranch house was to be our family's home for the next
fifteen years until the structure itself was moved to the hillside to
make way for the lake formed by the construction of Wells Dam ten
miles downstream.

My riparian adventures had begun earlier mid August when
Dad's future boss invited the family to the ranch for a trial orientation. The Crane house, a large two story with a covered porch
riverside, sat in the midst of a vast lawn shaded mostly by random
apple trees. One tree in particular struck my fancy, a gravenstein
tree whose apples were ripe and seemed the size of pumpkins to my
eight year old eyes. I was to brag about those apples to my friends
and classmates as the biggest apples in the world. That gravenstein
(apple trees were called their varietal names, less the word "tree":
the macintosh, spitzenberg, etc.) ushered our family into a way of
life the center of which was the apple industry. (My first paying

job was thinning blossoms from that monstrous gravenstein tree in Crane's yard.) Our hostess served us applesauce made from those pumpkin-size apples. To this day a spoonful of gravenstein applesauce evokes a lawn cluttered with large, globe shaped apples beneath limbs laden with fruit that would burst with juice when you sank your teeth into their mottled flesh.

It was on the cusp of summer and fall that I began my adventure with the river. The frame I've chosen for my riparian recollections is a seasonal one, a journey that began for me in the fall of 1953. And through each season the Columbia River flows, showing its multiple faces, moods, and mysteries, each of which spelled wonderment then to an eight year old boy and never ceased to be a fascination to me in the years that followed.

The face of the Columbia has changed. The subsequent hydraulics of the Wells Dam hydroelectric project have turned a free-flowing, determined river into a lake environment. Where subsurface currents exploded and blossomed on the surface, causing a rowboat to spin off course, now algae blooms and millfoil beds foul the river, assaulting one's nose with a foul stench when water levels drop. Once vibrant and vital, this stretch of river now projects a placid face that does little more than reflect the blue Okanogan sky and serve as a playground for the spring gales that churn its surface. There has been much talk about tearing down the dams. I'm unsure of the wisdom of such a move. But this I know: the magical playground where a young boy roamed, explored and lived now sleeps beneath forty feet of glacial-blue water.

THE ISLAND

Eastern Washington experiences changes that mark the march of the seasons. Skeins of geese passing south brought in fall and winter on their tail feathers. Meadowlarks and swallows set the spring. Cottonwood gold was but a memory when the willows puffed forth chubby catkins and the apple trees furred with green. But our calendar was the river, its palate of colors, the flux of its moods, its inexorable western flow—and a landform we called "the island." Because of the river's fluctuating levels, the island had a Jekyll and Hyde geography. Sometimes it was a peninsula, though in miniature. (I imagine when viewed from the air, it must have seemed like Florida, less the panhandle). Sometimes it was an island; sometimes a presence marked only by the roiled surface of the river; sometimes gone altogether.

The geology of the island was granite, abraded smooth, rounded by moving waters. River cobbles formed the neck of the island, graduated to boulders, giving the head its elevation, and when the neck was submerged, creating the island proper. Natural forces, like glaciation or massive volumes of shifting water in the process of river building must have deposited the nest of boulders at its head. Only heavy machinery could have budged a dozen of these; others, smaller in mass, two or three boys, curious to discover what lay beneath, might shift them aside long enough to peer under.

In late spring the island, like Proserpine, would sink to a watery underworld and then in late summer to our delight emerge like some reborn Atlantis, darkly shining, slimy with river sludge, calling to us again. We swam to it, fished from it, blackened it with campfires and probably, boulders excluded, left no stone unturned to expose whatever secrets it kept. This curious landform was focal to our life on the river and along with the seasons gives structure to these recollections growing up riparian.

THE HOUSE ON THE RIVER

"And you really live by the river? What a jolly life!"
By it and with it and on it and in it," said the rat.
"It's brother and sister to me and aunts, and company
and food and drink, and (naturally) washing. It's my
world and I don't want any other. What it hasn't got is
not worth having, and what it doesn't know is not worth
knowing.

Lord! the times we've had together. Whether it's in
winter or summer, spring or autumn, it's always got its
fun and its excitements."

The River Rat
The Wind in the Willows

A pianist with the Chicago orchestra invested in agricultural
futures out west and entered a partnership, Unity Orchards, with
Francis Crane's father George. The musician Alfred Devoto wanted
to spend his summers near his investment and had the two story

house built in 1920. Intended only for summer recreation, the house was poorly insulated, the riverside all windows the length of the living room like one big bay window to command full view of the river. During the financial straits of the late 1920s Unity dissolved in bankruptcy and Devoto exited with it, leaving his summer house to other occupants.

In the great flood of 1948 the river invaded the first story of the summer home. Driftwood shattered the windows in the living room, allowing the current to flow freely through the lower story. There was joint tenancy in the house then: the Columbia River frolicked about in the lower story while the family occupying the home was displaced to the upper story, commuting to land and back by a rowboat, which they moored to the house.

When we moved to the house in 1953, the hardwood floors were still warped and buckled from the floodwaters. Though such severe flooding did not repeat while we lived in the house, the river did flood our basement twice. At night you could hear the water ripple and lap around the oil furnace. I could fish out my bedroom window onto the lawn below. Novelty was my only reward; I caught no fish.

I have noticed as the years pass the world seems to grow smaller. When I last visited our house after it had been moved from the river bank to safety beyond the lake formed by Wells Dam, the interior floor plan appeared to have shrunk. The living room where we occupied ourselves rolling marbles to each other across the floor—where the marbles seemed to roll forever—now seemed too confined for us to have spent hours at such a pastime. The floor plan was unchanged, living room commanding the most space on the main floor. A sun room through which we passed from front porch to living room faced west and again all window on the river side. Off the east end of the living room was a utility room, more glass, and the back porch. The dining room, sandwiched, as were we all at mealtimes, between the utility porch and the kitchen, was little more than a cubicle. The partition separating dining room and kitchen included a window (we called it "the passthrough") through which tableware and food were passed. At the rear, the upslope side of the house, were a laundry room, a bathroom, and Mom and Dad's bedroom.

A tiny porch off the laundry room allowed access to our trash and burn barrels, a circumstance which was in part responsible for its tragic history and an impromptu visit from the Brewster volunteer fire department. When he earned the responsibility of burning the family's trash, brother Kevin apparently lacked fuel to sustain one of the trash burning sessions. He decided to supplement the combustibles by using the dog's bed, a pillow with a leather bottom. After his repeated attempts to ignite the cushion failed, little brother restored the bed to its designated corner of the porch. That was the only time a fire truck came to our house on the river. The smoldering dog bed had ignited the floorboards beneath. The firemen quickly located the fire and doused the flames. Kevin's incendiary responsibilities were immediately revoked, and the dog slept elsewhere that night. (Smoke filled the house a second time, and again Kevin was to blame. He relieved himself down the furnace grate, cleared us from the house for nearly three hours until our nostrils no longer stung from the "fumigant" and it was safe to return.)

We climbed a narrow, dangerous staircase to our bedrooms. The stairs were hardwood and uncarpeted. There was not a one of us who hadn't tumbled down them at least once. (I was in the routine of rushing the descent by leaping the last three steps to the landing, that is until I jumped too high, hitting my head on the stairwell overhang, slamming myself into the steps as if I had been pole axed. As I lay moaning on the stairs, I came to the painful awareness I must have grown another inch.) Kevin, our youngest sibling and the lightest, seemed to average one unorthodox descent a week, a muffled cacophony as if someone had dumped a sack of soup bones down the pitch, sending everyone rushing to the scene to search for survivors. (Whenever Kevin's fractious behavior exasperated us, Dad would urge tolerance, saying, "The poor little guy, you know—all those falls down the stairs..."). Christmas was the only time that wooden gauntlet proved friendly, when we huddled on them Christmas morning in the dark, waiting on tenterhooks for the signal to attack our presents.

Three bedrooms and a bathroom made up the second story floor plan. We would exchange bedrooms periodically for various reasons. Once I bunked in the bedroom where the floors were lino-leum so I could swab them clean of allergens daily to help control my allergies and asthma. Knotty pine boards paneled two of the bedrooms' walls. One of the boards in Tim and Kevin's room was missing a knot, causing concern that at night in the dark, "things" would creep into their bedroom to do them harm. (Plugging the hole with a rag somewhat allayed their fears, but still there was the chance....)

Tunneled into its bowels on the riverside of the house was a root cellar—or at least that's where we stored the apples we gleaned each fall after harvest. More likely the cellar was dug to install an oil furnace when year round use made it necessary to heat the poor-ly insulated house. This cellar was little more than a shoveled out trench wide enough to make room for the furnace. In this animal-musky tunnel—"the basement"—we stored our bikes when it rained or snowed; cats littered their kittens here; and twice while we lived on the riverbank, the river itself filled the basement.

In the fall rats would abandon the riverbank for the cellar. We could see them scurrying back and forth along the back foundation like tin ducks in a shooting gallery. At night we would hear them rattling along inside the walls as if they were ball bearings in a pin-ball machine or scuttling across the floors, sliding around corners, thumping into things. They would scurry up the plumbing to the upstairs bathroom, creep out from beneath the bathtub and terror-ize us in the dark. One night when I went to use the toilet, I turned on the bathroom light and exposed a rat gnawing an apple it had hauled up from the basement. For the next two nights I crouched under the sink cradling the .410, chambered with a shot shell cus-tomized with rock salt and barley grains. I waited in the dark pa-tiently, scarcely breathing, until at last I heard the scraping of fur against the wall and then the soft "plop" of a squat body on the floor.

I fired at the sound, then quickly switched on the light. No bleeding and kicking body, only flecks of blood on the floor and wallboard. I'd drawn blood but had no trophy to show for it.

I've heard stories of rats gnawing off noses, ears, and digits of infants as they slumbered in their cribs. I know one night a rat leaped on brother Tim's bed only to be launched forcefully into the dark by flailing feet and flying covers. Tim was not to be gnawed upon. Shivering with fright he spent the remainder of the night in my room. We tried traps but the rats avoided them—and poison—but I don't recall finding any dead rats about. Rats continued to plague us, some falls worse than others, all the years we lived on the river.

A sloping lawn surrounded the perimeter of the house, hard to mow, especially with the old push mower. A summer home needed no garage. One was never built at the house on the river. Our cars braved the weather year around, even the 1957 Chev Bel Air stationwagon, our family's first new car. Separating the front lawn from lower lawn, the driveway ended nearly at our front door, and the cars were always parked there. The front lawn was a triangle formed by the driveway and an orchard road that forked off above. At the apex of the triangle was an apple tree, an old common Delicious. Our house formed the base of the triangle.

Cloudless nights in Eastern Washington present a celestial swarm of stars in a vast, unpolluted sky. In those days I was passionate about astronomy. Stretched out on the front lawn on warm spring nights, I would plot the planets, stars, constellations on large sheets of newsprint: the Big Dipper, the North Star, Orion and the Pleiades, Venus, the Evening Star. Using a sky-to-paper scale to represent the distance between these pinpoints of light, I plotted my charts by visually approximating the black space between them and spacing their positions on the sheets of paper accordingly. My charts were rather like large negatives of the nighttime sky: the stars black dots, the distance between them white spaces of newsprint. By accident I found there was a second visual dimension to my sky charts. Using the lawn as a drawing board provided at best a springy surface on which to rest my pencil point. The pressure needed to mark the paper usually caused the tip to penetrate the newsprint. If I'd have thought to backlight my charts and project them upon a white wall, I could have created a crude planetarium, a money-making concern if I'd have charged my family admission. Inspired by the beauty and mystery of the freckled sky, I even tried to plot the courses of two or three meteors but had to abandon this activity as the newsprint always ripped.

The Comet

One winter a comet paid a visit to the night sky, wedged its way among the stars in the northwest heavens. It appeared as a whitish smudge on the carbon sky as if, I believed, it were a thumbprint made by something immortal, some being more awesome than all I knew. I pulled off the shelf the "C" volume from our *Encyclopedia Britannica* and read about comets. What I learned: that comets were little more than frozen gases massed to form the head, the tail a lesser concentration of dispersed ice particles–the whole works projected by solar illumination–did not do justice to the phenomenon. What I saw each night seemed to me considerably more: a living thing, animate like a stray cat or dog that shows up on your doorstep and stays. Knowledge is a fine thing but not without its disappointments.

The comet, of course, was invisible by day. I could not think about it in daytime without a slight sense of uneasiness, feared that when night came, the comet would be gone forever. It was as if the comet and I had formed a bond, a boy and his personal celestial friend. But come night there it would be, a comforting blemish reaching out to me from among the stars.

Sometimes after midnight when the rest of the household dreamed, I would awaken as if to a beckoning voice and make my way to the window to commune with the comet. Always a welcome sight it was to see my comet poised there above the black river among the shimmer of stars, my sole companion in the night; and I was not alone, as if the comet were a heavenly nite light, a comfort against the dark.

As the earth tilted toward spring, the comet slipped nightly toward the horizon, nearer the brow of the black hill beyond the river. I knew the comet's journey through deep space, even by light of day, continued, and as with all long distance relationships, ours, too, was destined to end. One night in early spring, the inevitable farewell. I arose in the dark, made my way to the window, and searched the northwestern horizon for the familiar blur. But the comet was gone, dropped behind the mass of hill. Just the lonely stars presented. I had read about comets, those icy astronauts of the solar system, frozen denizens traversing deep space. I knew in this lifetime I would never see mine again.

Landscape design had not been a priority in the overall scheme of the building site, nor did our move to the riverbank add much to the existing scheme. A few soft fruit trees, rose bushes, and some blue spruce were the sum of our involvement in landscaping the grounds. The front yard boasted a lilac bush and riverside of the front porch a large Mock Orange. Though its delicate fragrance seemed innocent enough, that bush scarred me for life. Years later in an educational seminar we were taught a technique to use in group work with students. Students were to show their partner a scar and then share the blood and gore story behind it. I immediately thought about a summer day, chores, the Mock Orange bush, and my right armpit.

Each year Dad pruned the Mock Orange, lopped off last year's growth flat top style so the new growth would not obscure the view from the sunroom windows. The traditional pruning reduced the bush to a height of six or seven feet. One summer's day, before I was released to my daily adventures, I was assigned the task of washing the sunroom windows next to the Mock Orange. I chose not to use a ladder for my work but balance instead on the narrow, slanted window ledge. I should have had the good sense to recognize that such precarious footing was sure to court disaster.

But providence seldom suffers fools, no matter what their age, and after a few swipes with the wash cloth, I tumbled from the ledge. The Mock Orange broke my fall. The next thing I knew, I was suspended in the bush, impaled in the pit of my right arm by one of the lopped branches. As I struggled to free myself, I spun on the branch, auguring the stub deeper into the flesh. I tried to push myself up and off the branch but had no leverage: my feet dangled a foot or so from the ground. Wrapping both legs around the limbs of the shrub and pulling upward with my left arm, I was finally able to lift myself up and off the branch. I dropped to the ground screaming in pain. My howls of distress brought Mom almost immediately. An examination of the injury showed it to be a puncture wound an inch deep or more. The injury assured me a trip to the doctor to have the wound cleaned (strangely enough there was little, if any, bleeding). I would most likely be given a shot for tetanus because....well, who knew what deadly bacteria the stub injected into my armpit?

As if my injury weren't trouble enough, my adventure had only begun. If my accident had happened the summer before or next year, Mom would have loaded me into the car and whisked us the four miles to the Brewster Clinic. This summer, however, the highway department was replacing the road deck of the Brewster Bridge, an old, trestle-style structure that spanned the Columbia River and allowed travelers to continue east or west on State Highway 173. (In 1968 in a similar resurfacing project, the bridge was totally destroyed by fire, accidentally ignited by a welder's torch.) Workmen would replace a ten or fifteen foot section a day, allowing traffic to cross before and after the day's work shift. In the meantime the bridge had a gap somewhere in the middle of its quarter mile span. To get to town, Mom would have to escort me across the bridge on foot via the wooden pedestrian walkway.

The Brewster Bridge terrified me. It spanned the river at a height of sixty feet; it trembled when traffic passed; the planks on the wooden footpath shifted under one's feet; and it was a long, long way across. (I'm not sure I had ever crossed the bridge on foot before that day. Alone, once I had tried but turned back after a third of the way, lacking the courage to continue any further). When Mom urged me onto the wood foot path, there was more throbbing than just my arm. At the worksite the road deck gaped; there was nothing between us but a sixty foot drop to the green water swirling around the support pillars; there was no reassuring handrail on the road side of the footpath. Giddy with fear and pain, a morbid thought came to me: what if I suddenly had the urge to jump into the void? I saw my body spinning down, down, growing smaller as it plummeted, arms and legs flailing the air. A splash and then my body disappeared beneath the swirling green. The errant though passed instantly, but I trembled the entire rest of the way—or at least till we were no longer over water.

The rest of the affair I hardly remember: the doctor, the cleansing and dressing of the wound. But, yes, there was the shot for tetanus; my arm ached from the injection for days it seemed, long after the pain left the injury. It is curious how two senses stimulated can evoke a third: to this day the sight or fragrance of Mock Orange sets my right armpit atingle.

Riverside, the long and narrow lawn was our main play area. The least lawn was the sparse, weedy patch behind the tiny porch on the upslope side of the house. Years of stove oil spillage (the fuel oil tank for the furnace was buried there) made the soil sterile. A clothes line stretched the length of the backyard, which was an adventure to mow when there were sheets on the line, maneuvering the mower up and down through canyons of sheets, my nose regaled by the fragrance of breeze-dried laundry.

A lone cottonwood tree separated the backyard from the lower lawn. By hauling up a few boards, some used for climbing rungs, we built a crude platform we called our treehouse. Though not much taller than the roof peak of our house, the perch was lofty enough to us, and we would use it as a lookout or for various games, as an escape from the commonplace, a loft to elevate both our fancy and our thoughts, a remove from the world of adults. Just like the pioneer forefather Daniel Boone used a tree to chronicle his dispatch of a bear, ("D. Boone killed a bar on this tree,") I used the old cottonwood trunk to record personal romance of another sort. With Boy Scout knife in hand and young love in my heart, I carved a crude heart into the gray bark and gouged at its center the initials "T" + "E." In this romantic equation the "T" stood, of course, for the initial of the carver's first name, and the "E" for the object of his prepubescent crush, Evonthea Daniels—or Evon as my fourth-grade classmates and I called her. Evon was my first serious love in the fourth grade and my new school. During the infrequent diversion of an educational film I held her hand throughout, oblivious to the message (a health film, I believe,) long enough to feel a moist intimacy, not the least unpleasant, when my hand shifted for a better grip of hers. To a fourth grader, focus on just about any subject was short—even serious affairs of the heart—and I remember no further details of intimacy or the duration of my crush, though I'm sure it did not see marble season, or, more to the point, was most likely terminated by it.

That is not to say Evonthea disappeared from my schoolyard experience. Somehow over the summer between fourth and fifth grade Evon developed breasts, the first girl in my class to do so. On the school ground the first day of fifth grade, news of my former flame's metamorphosis ran the gamut of the schoolyard grapevine and was the hot lunchroom topic for at least the first week of school. Evon continued in the vanguard of puberty for the next two years during which her bosom blossomed so prodigiously it was a delight to chase her just to set her torso in motion. And as the years passed, the old cottonwood tree and the inscribed heart continued to conjure up visions of a giggling and jiggling Evonthea disappearing around the corner of the school building pursued by a pack of boys trailing dust and desire.

The riverbank below the house sloped even more for approximately a hundred feet and then plummeted twenty more to the riverbed. This slope was not irrigated (except during the high water months in the summer) and only sparse grasses, snakeweed, asparagus bushes, cottonwood and willow copses grew in the dry, rocky soil. We had worn a path through this stretch of bank straight down to a fallen cottonwood tree, the roots of which had most likely washed loose during high water, toppling the tree. Its trunk lay across the path, parallel to the river, just where the bank pitched sharply down to the water. We called this landmark "The Old Dead Tree," a slight misnomer because the tree was not dead but nourished by enough root system to sustain sprouts and some sparse new growth near the top. Someone had nailed three or four boards to the top end of the trunk. To what purpose is not clear, for sitting or standing on the boards was hardly an adventure as they were scarcely a foot off the ground. You could produce a nice springboard effect by bouncing on the boards; there was some entertainment in that.

A river, any body of water, is a fascination to a child, but having one at one's doorstep (or literally in the cellar) is an extreme hazard if the child is a non-swimmer, which I was until the age of ten. Therefore certain mandates were in place to keep my siblings and me from washing up miles downstream, swollen like watermelons in the hot summer sun. We were not to go to the river unless in the company of an adult. The Old Dead Tree marked the boundary of our riverside exploits. To venture beyond and be caught was sure to bring swift retribution, either corporal in nature or restrictive (having our acres of playground reduced to the real estate of the yard proper for an entire week).

I only countered this edict once. One day while I was playing on the bank by The Old Dead Tree, I heard splashing from the river below and looked down to see some leviathan, some Ogopogo or "Nessie" cavorting and frolicking in the shallows. Believing this marvel to be a once in a lifetime sighting—a grounded sturgeon, perhaps—I felt fully justified to investigate this rarity of nature and dashed down the bank to the shore. Whether my appearance frightened the beast or its business was finished, I'm not sure, but the moment I came to a halt, the splashing stopped. Whatever caused the commotion and tempted the young, non-swimmer to stray off limits was gone. Only ripples remained, validating that I had not just imagined the event. Then all was calm—except for me. In the excitement of the moment I felt this was an experience I needed to share with Mom, hoping the incident proved marvelous enough to waive the out-of-bounds edict. Oh, the optimism of youth! No such luck. And though Mom listened with interest, the mandate prevailed. I believe I chose the shoe brush: the sudden whack, the stinging buttocks—a moment of pain was preferable to the confines of the yard for the eternity of a week. Malfeasance aside, one thing proved true: in all the days I spent beside, on, or in the river, that experience remained unique.

FALL

Shed of snowmelt, the turmoil of spring and summer over, the river languishes within its banks, complacent, reflecting the easy blue sky of shorter days. The island is fully peninsular, has been for several weeks. The backwater in its lee lies placid. Gnats in shifting clouds hover above this serene stretch of river, golden hordes in the western light.

Fall's first rain droops, drips down limb to twig to autumn parched earth, and there distills a heady fragrance from bush, from grass, from sage, mostly sage, the pungency of the sage.

I was the new kid that fall in the third grade in a new school with a new teacher, Miss Newton, a sturdy, middle-aged woman much the bearing and appearance of the British comedian Dame Edna, though a bit more masculine. She was bent over a student's desk assisting with the lesson when I, hovering close to Mom's side, was introduced. Miss Newton turned to greet us. The woman had a broad face and a mouth enclosed by palsied lips which contended for control of her face. Her lower lip did battle with the upper, rising to meet it like the crest of a wave. When she spoke the battle subsided. Only more impressive than her leonine head was the fact that as she turned, she broke wind for what seemed to me an amazing length of time.

Beyond this cheerful introduction I have distinct memories about my third grade teacher. The first was her interest in vulcanology and the visual aid she prepared to show us the principles of volcanic action and mountain building. On a small sheet of plywood, Miss Newton built a papier-mache miniature of a volcanic cone. For the cone's crater, she imbedded a small baby food jar. To simulate an eruption, Miss Newton packed the glass crater to the rim with some orange crystals, rock-salt size. When she ignited the crystals, the cone shot flames, and green ash spewed from the maw of the cone, spilling down its sides. After a few demonstrations, the ash covered the cone, enlarged it in much the same way lava, ash, and pumice expand the girth of the real thing. For optimum effect Miss Newton would darken the room, ignite the project. The crater would hiss and spit sparks: we couldn't have been more impressed had we been in the presence of a Vesuvius or Mauna Loa. Today, no doubt, such a lesson would be forbidden, as I'm sure the gases, Miss Newton's excepted, emitted in the process would most likely be noxious to a young audience.

Miss Newton also introduced me to and helped me acquire three children's classics: *The Adventures of Tom Sawyer*, *Heidi*, and *Treasure Island*, which she encouraged her students to purchase. Though we waited eagerly for their arrival, the books failed to show, arrived sometime over the summer, an enticement for us to return that fall to the fourth grade. I still own those three volumes.

School was not where I wanted to be those crisp, gilded days of September. Not that I didn't like the classroom, but in those days I had a riverbank to explore. Off the bus, rush home, change into my "work" clothes, slip my Boy Scout knife in my pocket and head for the riverbank and the nearest cottonwood sapling. I had discovered the satisfying craft of wood carving, and the soft cottonwood was just the right medium for a young craftsman with a dull Scout knife. I loved the smell emanating from the bark, the sharpness of turpentine as I shaved it to expose the white, gleaming wood beneath. Hacking off a foot long section, I would lie on my back and carve shaving after shaving away, shaping the stick. My works in progress were always canoes, the perfect project for the young whittler.

Once the bark was stripped, half the work was done. Choose the side I wanted to be the keel, carve away the top half, round the ends to make a prow and stern, and the craft was nearly complete. Hollowing away the innards was a challenge. The single blade was butter knife dull and the point nearly as round as either end of my canoe. I usually concluded with a product decidedly concave but splintered and uneven. In spite of my efforts, none of these cottonwood craft took to the water like the real thing. At launch time, concurrent with my evening bath, each maiden voyage ended with the canoe of the day either turning turtle or bobbing gunwales awash. But no matter. That first September I spent my after school hours with my Scout knife amid the cottonwood, blissfully whittling away until dusk. At the call to supper I would close the blade into its handle, brush the fragrant shavings from my black silk jacket with the Japanese dragon embroidered on the back (a gift from my Uncle Mike, who was in the Air Force and always remembered the nieces and nephews with exotic trinkets from overseas), and come the nightly bath, launch yet another failure.

Harvest

Fall is a reckoning time of the year
When the stock of the summer is brought up to clear.

Fall brought harvest and excitement to the riverbank. Tasks that began with the first swollen bud in April—and they were legion—now yielded acres of trees pendulous with fruit, fruit to be picked, sorted, packed, refrigerated and shipped with haste: but a careful and precise haste. The routine pace of the work day, the week, ratcheted up to a seven day, non–stop bustle. Every hour took on a sense of anxiety, of rush and hurry. There was urgency in the air; you could smell it in the tractors' spewed exhaust, see it on the face of every worker (with the first pear harvested, Dad donned his "harvest face," an expression taut with an intensity he sustained until the cold storage doors clacked shut on the last packed box); you could feel the urgency on every laden branch, propped against the burden of red and yellow globes of fruit, an urgency for release from weight. Pickers, harnessed into buckets, set ladders and clambered up into the fruit. When the bucket heaped, the picker eased his way down rung by rung, one arm cradling the bulging mouth to keep the contents from spilling. Leaning low over the wooden box, he loosed the knotted ropes, released them from the metal basket, and slowly, oh, so gently he stood and the apples glided neatly into the box. One bag per box, back to the ladder, repeat the routine—for a good picker 200 to 250 times a day, from tree to box and back from the dew of dawn till the picking boss said quit the field.

Men called "swampers" lugged the laden boxes from the fields, box after box from ground to trailer, unloading them again at the packing shed where the fruit was wheeled into cold storage rooms for rapid chilling. Swampers worked during twilight and dark, for all fruit harvested during the day had to be swamped out and refrigerated to prevent spoilage. Dust kicked up of a harvest day lingered in the autumn air, in the evening hung like a pall over the river as the sun slipped west toward Billygoat Mountain. The tractors roared into the dusk.

Cooled fruit began its journey through the packing line, first washed, then sorted and graded by three grades according to size and color: *Blueline*, top of the line, *Redline*, quality somewhere in the middle, *Greenline*, third class produce, yet suitable for packing. Bruised, punctured, misshapen or watercored fruit was culled out to be processed into juice. Individually wrapped (except for *Greenline* grade), and tucked firmly into pine boxes, new and clean–scented, the packed boxes coasted on rollers to the nailing machine to be lidded. The machine operator glued and slapped labels on both ends of each box, which the rollers returned to the cold storage to await shipment.

Fruit in the modern orchard is harvested in bins, large crate-like containers that hold nearly a ton of fruit, but when we lived on the river, pickers filled one box at a time. It took thousands of boxes to clear a season's worth of fruit from the fields. These field boxes were stored in large piles of 20,000 or more individual units, in nests of three: two per end and one stashed between. I have reason for such detail because one fall these apple boxes provided us an unusual diversion, an adventure involving commonplace orchard fauna, namely mice. I'll call this rodent experience "The Great Mouse Roundup," how that fall we thusly became "Mouseketeers."

An important pre-harvest ritual was the distribution of the apple boxes throughout the orchards. Experienced workers would size up each tree, estimate its approximate yield, and stack that number next to the tree: "This one'll pick sixty-five, that one eighty...," leaving the boxes dormant until pickers moved to the fields. In the interim these stacks attracted myriads of orchard mice seeking winter refuge beneath the layers of pine slats. Moving their families into the spaces under the box pile, they immediately began burrowing an elaborate network of runs and tunnels. After about two weeks each stack was a scurry of mice, a tenement of entire rodent populations. The poet Robert Burns observed, "The best laid plans of mice and men go oft astray," and for these refugees from the vast orchard spaces the statement proved true indeed. These mice metropolises were destined to be dismantled come harvest when the boxes were to house apples, not mice, and would be put to that purpose, creating an exodus of displaced pilgrims when the bottom tier was dislodged. I'm sure the pickers, whose livelihoods depended on picking fruit and picking it fast, paid little attention, if any, to the fleeing creatures. However, my playmates and I did, and our evictions precluded those of the pickers.

Donning gloves—because the little critters had needles for teeth and an aversion to being handled, a combination guaranteed to draw blood—we would set about dismantling the piles. When we reached the last tier, we would plan our strategy. On a count of three each of us was to lift a nest of boxes and set it aside simultaneously. Once the signal was given, we dashed the boxes aside. Mice of all sizes exploded from the grass: field mice, sleek, streamlined, trailing tails longer than their bodies; meadow mice, short—tailed, squat of body, mole-like—oldtimers and youngsters alike dashed for the exits. Like hawks we were upon them, scooped them up in our gloved hands, and dropped their squirming bodies into a paper shopping bag.

On one mouse roundup we corralled sixty-five of the teeth-packing, furry varmints, had them layered and standing on each oth-er's heads in the sack. Else they gnaw their way to freedom, we shook the sack frequently to disallow those needle-like teeth a purchase on the paper walls. We headed home as triumphant as did Peter with his wolf, where I deposited the bagful of mice into a terrarium in my room and watched my frenzied prisoners until bedtime.

Late that night I awakened to a scratching sound and flipped on the lights to investigate. My room was alive with mice: mice on the bedspread, windowsill, mice skidding about on the linoleum floor, not a one willing to share the room with his captor. In vain I tried to recapture them, but they were too many and the terrarium apparently not to their liking. Finally I left them alone and returned to bed after carefully checking the bedclothes to avoid double bunk-ing with a needle-toothed bedfellow. Next morning there was not a mouse to be seen; the entire bagful had vanished to parts unknown, most likely fled to the adjacent orchard to reestablish another box pile tenement.

Harvest brought not only new routines to ranch life but also new faces. Families whose limited means dictated a migrant lifestyle came for harvest, following the fruit to supplement a meager income (my girlfriend Evonthea and her family were among these itinerant families). Many of these migrant families had homes in Oklahoma and Arkansas but made the annual trek to the orchards of the northwest each fall where long hours at harvest wages and the seasonal bonus (if they stayed the season) would be sufficient to sustain their families until they could find work the following year.

The peregrinations of these families I accepted without question, never learning much about their lives beyond the ranch. Whenever they left, usually at whim and a moment's notice, I was not curious to learn where they went, or lived, or how they led their lives in that distant world that called them back.

Sometimes these families stayed year round for two or three years before the South called them back. Their children were our playmates, schoolmates, and seatmates on the school bus. Mickey Schultz, the younger son of the Williams family, was my best friend off and on from the sixth grade to our freshman year. The Williams had a TV, an innovation my parents and the Cranes considered a frill. After school I would change clothes and rush back to Mickey's house in time to watch the Mickey Mouse Club show. In those days I was not only in love with TV, but also the captivating Annette Funicello who sported a Mouseketeer's pair of mouse ears, the ever present angora sweater, and a pair of something else, creating pleasing contours beneath. When Annette introduced herself, "Hi, I'm Annette," Mickey and I would make suggestive noises and feign to swoon with passion. Miss Funicello had no more loyal fans than Mickey and I and our adolescent glands.

When they had to be away, though such occasions were infrequent, Mom and Dad would request the babysitting services of Mickey's mother Blanche ("Mrs. Widyums," we kids called her). The Williams seemed stable—my friend Mickey seemed normal enough—but there were behaviors our conventional family considered foreign. Mickey, for instance, had a step-father, Tex, Blanche's second or third husband. And Blanche, a tall, rangy woman who walked with a gangly, disjointed gait, her voice husky from cigarettes, once displayed a behavior I thought strange.

One day at Mickey's house—I believe we were engaged in play that took us inside and out—I noticed Blanche kneeling before a bedroom window as if she were peering out at something. At first I gave the scene little thought, but then I noticed she had not parted the curtains but had inserted herself between them and the window so they hung down her back like a cape. The curtains were sheer, so I could see her motionless form silhouetted against the windowpane. Periodically she would lift her hands to her head, fuss about her face, drop her hands again and repeat the procedure. I was curious, wanted to see from without what she was doing with or to her face, though I knew it would be an impropriety to investigate. My friend seemed nonplussed by his mothers' behavior. When I asked him what she was doing, he replied that she had some sort of condition and dealt with it in this manner. I accepted the vague explanation, let it go at that; besides, we had a game going. To this day I have no idea why she communed with the window.

One Saturday Blanche and Tex put on a show that had the entire camp in an uproar. Much to Tex's dismay, Blanche, inspired by the bottle, barricaded herself in one of the pickers' cabins with another man and refused to come out. Tex would have her out or else. The noisy standoff lasted well into the evening, until the liquor wore off—or ran out, and Blanche shuffled forth of her own volition. Noisy recriminations followed, but that seemed the extent of the few hours' estrangement, the issue apparently being more about spousal obedience than soiled goods. Mickey's parents continued their strange relationship for several years, I believe; however, I can't remember any further babysitting services being required of Blanche after her public Saturday frolic.

While we lived on the river, six separate families, including the Williams, lived in my friend's house: the Morleys (Ozzie Morley and I were blood brothers, had scratched our wrists and mingled blood), the Whites, the Shenyers, the Petersons and the Warfords. The Warford family held the longest tenancy. Elmer and his wife Zona had eight children: Clyde, Dixie, Claude, Doris, Darlene, Billy, Betty, and Dorothy. Elmer fancied himself a lady's man (probably was in his younger days) and on the weekends, dressed in his Sunday clothes, his hair slicked back, cast a roving eye about camp, looking for prospects. Zona kept one eye on her husband's whereabouts and the other squarely on God, sin, and redemption. To my knowledge Elmer's philanderings were mostly fantasy; any advances he made (for certain there was one) were brusquely spurned, yet he always persisted, ever hopeful his imagined chemistry would bring him "lady" luck.

Returning to the ranch one spring, nearly the entire Warford family was killed in a terrible car crash in southern Idaho. Billy, the youngest son, cushioned by the bodies of his sisters, was the only survivor. I had worked alongside Elmer many times, listened to his stories, most of which began: "I once knowed a feller...." Claude and I were hunting partners, and though his dad was skilled with firearms, Claude lacked the quick reflexes necessary to be a first rate shotgunner. Now both were dead, crushed to death in Claude's turquoise Ford Galaxy, his pride and joy. But the death of Darlene, the middle daughter, staggered me.

Spring, two years before, Darlene was fifteen and I seventeen and we were boyfriend and girlfriend. Ours was the typical teenage romance, as intense as it was short lived, enhanced in our case by vernal stimulation, the greening of leaf and bud, warmed by a young spring sun. I could not comprehend that Darlene, a girl I had embraced, kissed, with whom I had shared intimate moments, was now cold and still, somewhere far away covered with earth. I would never see her again. I remembered the love notes she wrote me, sealed and sealed again with a blotch of lipstick (freshened I'm sure, for the occasion), and secreted away in a place known only to us. Darlene—our moments alone, necking in my old Ford truck, fishing together at Alta Lake (I made her wear a life jacket because she couldn't swim), and down at the river in those days of May when the whitefish were jumping. Now she was dead, her body mangled in Claude's blue car. Grief was a new experience to my heart.

The Gragg family, Virgil, his wife Eva and two sons, Mervyn and Dennis, lived on the Crane Ranch nearly as long as my family.

Mervyn, two years my senior, had interests and talents not common with mine, but Dennis and I were the same age, loved sports, especially basketball, which we played at school or on the dirt court behind the cookhouse garage and storage shed. If we were not shooting around, playing "horse" or "pig," engaged in a game of one-on-one, we were playing marbles. I liked Dennis. He was carefree and easy-going but most of all eager to take on whatever adventures I was. We were friends and playmates for years on the river.

When they first came to the ranch, the Graggs lived in a three room clapboard cabin behind Cranes' house. The cabin had no indoor plumbing, and the family had to use an outdoor facility a few yards from their doorstep in the surrounding orchard. The Graggs lived in that ramshackle cabin three or four years until Virgil earned seniority enough to move to a more comfortable dwelling, one with more rooms—and indoor plumbing—the house opposite Ernie Whitley's, on the edge of the orchard planting we called the "80." Graggs' new home was a mile away from ours, which meant either Dennis or I had to walk home if we wanted to play together after school.

If you looked about you on the riverbank, you were apt to see amazing sights. That was how I came to see my first naked woman. The naked lady was Mrs. Gragg, my friend's mother. I think I was ten or eleven at the time. The incident was as surprising as it was innocent. I mention it here because it was the most singular thing my eyes had ever seen and to this day remains among the strangest.

Sunday was the only day of rest on the ranch, and Sunday mornings the entire camp slept late, even our family. The riverbank offered too much adventure for one to loll about in bed, and Sunday mornings I was up and out the door early, careful not to wake the family. I would slip from the house and venture out to see what the world had to offer. On such a Sunday I made my way through the quiet morning to the Graggs' cabin to see what my friend and his family were up to. As I mentioned earlier, the cabin consisted of three rooms in a line—one long rectangle—each separated by a wide doorway, though without doors, open from one end to the other. The first room served as both kitchen and living room; the second functioned as bedroom; the third, storage. The front room had one window through which one could view the entire length of cabin in a single glance. Through this window I peered that Sunday on the lookout for any Gragg activity.

I had visited my friend's cabin numerous times, played there—had even shared lunch a time or two and was well aware that Dennis's family was not like my own. I knew this because in the spare room stacked on a table were two or three large cardboard boxes piled high with crusts of bread and toast, several loaves worth at least. I've heard of people—families—who having fallen on hard times, later horded food should the lean times return. Perhaps the Graggs were laying by the basics just in case. I have no idea why I did not ask my friend about this humongous cache of toast. At my age I'm sure I accepted this oddity as simply curious and let it pass. I stood on tiptoe and peered into the cabin. At the far end, framed in the doorway, surrounded by crusts and slices of toast, stood a naked woman brushing her hair. I was so startled I could do nothing but stare. There she stood, my friend's mother, facing me, serenely pulling a brush stroke by stroke through her frizzled hair, while her family and the toast slumbered around her. I knew it was a sneaky thing to do, to stare, to invade her privacy. I knew there would be severe consequences should I be caught. I knew, yet I could not take my eyes from her. Though it seemed like much longer, for ten or fifteen seconds I ogled. Then she placed her brush on the table beside the heaps of bread, and while her gaze was averted, I ducked and ran.

To this day, when I retrieve the image it returns as vivid and lovely as on that Sunday morning. Mrs. Gragg—Eva—would hardly be considered a comely woman. Of Portuguese descent, Dennis's mother was short, olive-skinned, and as today's newspaper personals state: height/weight proportional. Unclothed she was beautiful, with small, firm breasts, every soft curve set in motion by the deliberate stroking of her hair. To me she was not Mrs. Gragg—Eva—but Eve—the first—my first—naked woman. Now that I know something of art, Eva could have been the nude subject of Gauguin, from his Polynesian period, hers the soft, graceful curves of a Tahitian beauty. Yet the incongruity of a nude in the presence of boxes heaped with singed toast had something Boschian about it as well. Had either artist painted the scene, I wonder at their titles: Gauguin, "Nude with Hairbrush"; Hieronymous Bosch, "Nude Among Crouton Delights." But to me the vision, strange though it was, was poignant and lasting. Of course over the years I saw Mrs. Gragg often when I went to play with Dennis, but clothed she was just the mother of my friend, separate entirely from my vision, my beautiful Queen of Crusts.

The Woolies of Fall

On a fall afternoon a cloud of dust moved slowly up river from Pateros on the opposite river bank. I knew what caused the cloud, what stirred the river bank dust—sheep, a flock a thousand or so strong. They had come down from the Methow Valley high country where they had pastured that summer, grazing in the high mountain meadows. Sheep in large numbers were a curiosity to us. By late afternoon the flock had reached the bank opposite our house. A large flock of sheep creates not only dust but a stir of sound as well. The sound carried well across the water: the guttural baas, the hollow gonging of the bells on the bellwether leaders, the whistles and cries of the drovers. The flock would be the first of two driven upriver to be herded across the Brewster Bridge to Douglas County and up the primitive road past the Whitley place to Dyer Hill to winter in the wheat fields.

In the years the bands traveled the riverbank (in later falls the sheep were trucked to their winter quarters), the entire congregation bedded down and camped the night opposite our house. It was then we were treated to a spectacle that left us awestruck no matter how many times we witnessed it—the miracle of the sheepdog at work in the field.

Never more than a pair of herders tended the large flock en route to winter pasture. This number was most likely superfluous because of the dogs, usually three, though on occasion four. From our vantage point across the river this mob of sheep appeared as some large organism, like a lanolin amoeba pulsing beneath a microscope. Sheep, I believe, act on visceral, not cerebral impulses, evident in the way they progressed up river. Small bands—perhaps only a half dozen head or so—would lag behind; others moved to the water to drink; a few would be tempted by the lush grasses in the orchards several yards up the bank; some perched atop boulders, imitating their mountain goat cousins. If the mass of bodies shifted too far off course, black dots would dart out of nowhere at these prodigals, creating a flurry of activity among the wayward, who quickly blended into the fold. These lightning-quick forays apparently lacked command; the dogs knew when the troops had overstrayed their limits. We would marvel at the intelligence of these dogs, at the efficiency with which they went about their work. The dog versus sheep show continued throughout the evening, with the entire flock spread over two or three acres of riverbank. Then at dusk all the wandering nonsense ended. Whistles and commands from the shepherds set the dogs upon the sheep. Barking and nipping at the dumb beasts, they flanked and surrounded them. In less than five minutes the dogs compressed three acres of sheep into less than an acre, as if a well-flung canine lariat lassoed the entire flock into a near perfect circle of wooly backs. Then it was dark and a campfire winked among the rocks; only voices and an occasional tolling bell marked the spot where a thousand cuds churned in the night.

Our friends the Millers who owned an orchard across the river and lived beside the highway upbank from the sheep camp once visited the shepherds. They asked about the dogs, how long it took to train a good sheepdog. About three or four years, the drovers said, were necessary to produce a topnotch, sheepwise working animal. The shepherds said they had been offered as much as a thousand dollars for one of their dogs; their counter bid was a burst of laughter: you can't put a price on a helpmate and a friend.

No matter how early I arose, I don't ever remember seeing the sheep show break camp and continue up river. The next day, flock, shepherds, and dogs were nowhere to be seen, their predawn departure probably due to sharing the bridge with the morning traffic, not wanting to snarl the morning commute. Excepting a primitive road pocked by four thousand cloven hooves and peppered with sheep pellets, this ritual of fall passed nearly unnoticed.

Fire on the Island

"Nine p.m.: Do you know where your children are?" Look out the windows where the river runs dark, where an orange light flickers from the rocks, to the head of the island where flames tongue the night. A fire signals back because it is where we are. We have spent the afternoon combing the banks for driftwood fuel and hauling it to the fire site. Now we toss piece after piece on the coals. Sparks burst skyward, hang for a moment against the speckled heavens and wink out. The ring of light pulses outward, settling upon the rush of dark water, lifts the reflection beyond the top most rock, whirling it away into darkness. It is campfire night on the island.

Tonight's menu: hamburgers mottled and thick, now pressed between waxed paper sheets. These we unpack from the grocery bag along with the cast iron skillet. The condiments and buns perch precariously on the flattest rocks around the fire pit. Nestle the skillet in the coals and soon the patties are sizzling away. The medley of frying meat, cheery warmth against the evening chill, a fall sky huge with stars, the talking river around us, conspire against our hunger and patience. We pluck the sizzling meat from a pool of spitting grease and tuck the patties, singed or rare, inside a bun amid a slather of mustard, catsup and relish. We eat our fill, throw the leftovers to the fish, and sated for the moment, let the river and the night converse until the fire dims and the hour sends us home.

Sometimes we roast hotdogs on green willow withes cut from a thicket near the island. These were usually studies in crisp, black flakes we would strip to expose the pink, dripping flesh beneath.

Or camouflage with mustard or catsup, a splash of primary colors, if not pleasing to the palate, at least to the eye.

For dessert, delicate French fare: marshmallows flambeau, served en brochette a'la green willow branch. Here the presentation demanded a steady hand and a keen eye, the exact rate of rotation. One slip and the bubbling blend of browns, the coveted golden jacket poised above the coals would explode in flame. Then technique be damned. Wild stick flailings and frantic puffings, produced at best a "blown save." Oh, you could remove the black shroud and start afresh, but the white, gooey blob was a virgin sullied. Best to concede defeat, spear a new victim, and advance again to the coals. Mostly we would "smoor" the white mounds, nearly always singeing our fingers in the process.

My pinnacle achievement at island campfire cookery was wild game: mourning dove broasted in foil. September brought dove season, and once after bagging my limit of little bodies, I reduced them to ten mounds of flesh each the size and color of a child's fist. The tiny giblets I stuffed into each body cavity, which I primed with a pat of butter. I swaddled each breast in a strip of bacon, fastened the slice firmly in place by a toothpick, wrapped each delicate mound, as with potatoes, in foil, and headed for the island.

We spread the silver balls among the coals as if they were rare coins; later plucked the tarnished bundles from the fire and set them aside to cool. What exotic fare–the texture a bit rubbery, but the flavor delicate, the hint of smoke just enough to compliment the gaminess. We could have eaten ten apiece! A regal meal, but as was the case with the Egyptian queen who dined on hummingbird tongues, there was just not enough to go around.

When inspiration was upon us, we would concoct a mulligan stew, a recipe intended not for the gastronome but solely entertainment. Our specialty was crawdad mulligan. During the afternoon we would catch a half dozen crawdads and set them aside in a large coffee can. These fearsome little crustaceans we hunted in the shallows of the deep pool formed by the neck of the island.

They came in a variety of earth tone colors: some murky green or blue, some brown, some nearly black, others rust-like, the color of blood. All, after a boiling water bath, turned a brilliant lobster red.

Sometimes you might see one picking its way along the slimy cobbles, lumbering along like a miniature tank. In a rare instance you might discover a landlubber, usually a large specimen, high and dry among the rocks. But most of the time you had to hunt hard to find them, flipping over stone after stone before one shot out from beneath. We soon learned to take advantage of a crawdad's backward habits. Any frontal assault on the little shellfish (a crawdad's pincers, through impressive, seemed to offer little defense) would result in an equal but opposite reaction. A sudden downward flip of its fan-like tail and the threatened creature rocketed backward, usually into deep water, out of our reach.

Once we discovered the little critter's penchant for the reverse gear, it was a cinch to catch one. After you located your prey, you employed a stick and coffee can in the following fashion: the stick you used as a diversion, waggled it about in the water just beyond the creature's startle zone; then you submerged the coffee can, carefully slid it into position a foot or so behind Mr. Crawdad. Poke the stick and in defensive reverse it shot backwards into the can, which you quickly jerked from the water, leaving the little fellow to circle the bottom of his prison in a pout while you carried him to join his ill-fated brothers.

Next we gathered the fruits of the field: an apple, a pear, sweet plums and cluster or two of grapes from the small vineyard below Cranes' lawn. These we chopped up and added to the can of crawdads. At campfire time we would set the can in the fire, heat it until the contents frothed down the side into the fire. Using a shirt or a sock as a hot pad, we removed the mulligan, poked through the mush with a stick to locate the blushing crawdads. Satisfied the ingredients were thoroughly cooked, we then carried the can to the bank and dumped the contents into the river. I don't know why one of us didn't dare the other to sip the heady broth. Perhaps it was because a campfire buddy, in a brilliant flash of mulligan genius, once added his own highly personal touch to the evening's stew—a bladder full of urine, and produced a mulligan with a tremendous head on it, every bit equal to a premium batch of fire retardant foam. With mulligan cookery it was understood that no recipe would ever be repeated, and though there were no duplicates, every last one of them was taken to the river and flushed down current.

The island campfires met more than our culinary needs; I used them as an open kiln to fire the pottery I made from clay gathered at the clay banks in the canyon. I was inspired to create the clay bowls by one of the Straight Arrow "how-to" cards used in those days to separate the layers of biscuits in Nabisco shredded wheat breakfast cereal. One card showed how Indian potters rolled the clay medium into clay snakes, coiling one to make the bottom. The others were coiled one upon the other to make the sides. With wetted fingers and palms I would smooth out the coils, thus yielding a crude vessel any self respecting Indian artisan would have chucked on the scrap heap where it might be unearthed, marveled at, and studied centuries later by a zealous archaeologist. I was disappointed because my artifacts wouldn't hold water without returning to their initial stage of mush. A little research in the *Encyclopedia Britannica* taught me about kilns and fire-cured clay. And it was at this stage of clay craft the island campfire came in handy. My artwork emerged tinged with charcoal smears and tinges of pink, probably from the iron in the clay, and though primitive looking, they proved utilitarian at last: I could—and did boil water in them.

It was due to the Indian/pottery period of my artistic evolution that I had my only experience with pipe smoking. Again, it was a Straight Arrow craft card that inspired me, a card that featured an elaborate Indian ceremonial pipe, replete with feathers and other trappings. Off to the clay banks where I again gathered more clay, pulverized, dampened it, and fashioned a pipe bowl. With a sharp stick I reamed a hole in the damp clay to seat the pipe stem. I split a section of branch, scraped away its pithy center, glued the halves together again, and twisted the stem into the bowl. I had my pipe, and though it lacked the embellishments of Straight Arrow's, it looked like it would do the trick.

Now for the tobacco. Growing profusely on the riverbank was a weed we called "Indian tobacco," a plant whose seed stalks produced great quantities of green, paper-like seeds, each about BB-size. I'm sure the plant was as much akin to tobacco as a rosebush is to cactus. The seeds dried to a dark brown, tobacco colored. A handful, when stripped from the stalk, looked similar to the pipe tobacco Grandpa Johnson, a pinch at a time, extracted from a pouch to pack his pipe. With this handy surrogate I primed my crude meerschaum and headed to the depths of the orchard, spurred on by high adventure and the pack of matches in my pocket. I touched flame to the "tobacco," drew on the pipe stem, and my lungs filled. I had done my work well. A horrible smoke rushed in, and everything caught fire: my eyes, lungs, mouth, and tongue. I staggered home and was sick for three days, my fascination with things Indian considerably diminished. To this day I have never used a tobacco product and religiously believe I have my clandestine smoking experience, the "Indian tobacco," and the noxious fumes from my home made pipe to thank for my nicotine abstinence.

Duped and Devastated

Yes, in those days woodcraft and Indian lore fascinated me. In an old photograph I pose on the lower lawn, smile at the camera, and strike the warlike stance of a young brave. In my right hand I brandish a war club carved from apple wood. Girdling my loins is an old leather belt through which I have slipped a length of rayon cloth long enough to pass between my legs, cover my nether parts. The excess slopped over fore and aft, a breechclout, a loincloth—Indian garb. This getup I adorned with amber glass beads, which I strung on nylon fishing line and stitched to the fabric. My feet were shod in moccasins, faux buckskin, the pattern cut and stitched from Dad's castoff work khakis. Thus clad and barely decent, I would sprint around the yard, an Indian runner jogging through the forest primeval, a noble savage, sporting a crew cut.

Once or twice I took to the hills in this outfit, foraged for coyote berries, even found the nerve to crunch down a live grasshopper or two, live off the land in the manner of my red brothers. After an hour spent clambering on the rocks and crashing through the sagebrush, my legs would be scratched, bloodied, my feet stone bruised, moccasins reduced to tatters, khaki shredded, stitching undone. But regardless the hardship, my passion for the noble red man remained.

It was because of this adoration for things Indian I experienced one of my bitterest disappointments in the years I lived on the river. One day, due to some dam tinkering upstream, the river level dropped considerably, exposing yards of riverbank usually submerged. Treasure hunting at this low ebb would be at its best, so I set out to search among the slippery rocks along the river bar above Owl Thicket. I searched primarily for fishing gear: spinners—wobble-rites, we called them—and flatfish, lures that had lodged in the rocks, lost to some unfortunate fisherman. I knew their value; they were expensive to replace.

It was no wobble-rite I found among the slimy river cobbles but some kind of ring. I rinsed the muck from my find and examined it. About two and a half inches in diameter, the thickness of a pencil, the ring appeared to be fashioned from bone or so my archaeology determined. A three-notch design appeared at intervals around the ring, each notch rust-colored; obviously, I possessed primitive artwork. I thought I had unearthed an item of Indian jewelry, a bracelet, I imagined, which centuries before had adorned the slender brown wrist of some Indian princess. Now I knew in days passed, Indians had gone before, traversed these riverbanks, camped along them, passing from hunting ground to hunting ground. To find shards of flint and pottery, stone tools, broken arrow points cast off or left behind by some native artisan was quite common along the river. The Humborg brothers Larry and Don had collected a wonderful assortment of spear and arrow points, stone scrapers, beads and other artifacts, all screened from the sand bars of Bonita Flats, an old Indian encampment. But an Indian bracelet crafted of bone—a rare find indeed.

Clutching the precious artifact, I hurried home, anxious to share the discovery with the family, especially Dad. No sooner was he home from work and in the door than I showed him the bracelet. Dad examined the ring carefully, turned it over, felt its heft. To my surprise, he seemed skeptical of the artifact, questioned its authenticity. "What else could it be," I wondered, "lying there on the riverbank far from camp, far from any house or home?" That Dad should suggest otherwise seemed preposterous. Maybe we should consult some authority, one learned in Indian lore, I offered.

As it turned out, no sophisticated dating method—no Carbon 14 inquiry—was necessary. Dad proposed a simple proof: he would trim a sliver from the ring and apply the flame test. Bone would not burn; celluloid would: red man, no smoke; white man, heap fire. Dad sliced a sliver from the ring, set it on the counter, and struck a match. So desperately did I want the relic to be genuine, signify Indian presence on the river, I hardly dared watch. Dad pressed the flaming match against the sliver. It glowed, flared, then disappeared. And with that flash of flame, that puff of smoke, my heart broke. I burst into tears, fled to my room, was inconsolable for the evening. I had invested all my hopes in the ring and it had proved a fraud. Never had the ring graced the comely wrist of an Indian princess, but rather someone's shower stall, dangled from a shower rod, plastic support for someone's shower curtain.

Today I still wonder at my overreaction. Perhaps what for Dad was a simple test for knowledge I mistook for an act of cruelty. Perhaps I was angry at being duped. Most likely, though, as was the case even in those days, I could not bear being proved wrong.

The Harvest Dinner

On the ranch by the river the orchards were bare, as if some heavy booted army had marched through, crushing underfoot the orchard cover. Stripped clean but for frost-shocked leaves, the trees stood bewildered. The last wooden box swamped from the field, the last apple sorted, graded, wrapped and packed in a box labeled *Crane & Crane*, and chuted into the dark bowels of the cold storage shed.

Shed doors closed, the clanking machinery within stilled, loading docks deserted, and returned to the vendor the vending machine where you fed a dime in the slot, pulled a lever and like a chunk of firewood down crashed a *Payday* bar. The camp seemed to slumber, a boom town gone bust.

But not tonight. Tonight an animated crowd milled about the cookhouse doors. The crisp evening air commingled with the aroma of the harvest feast wafting from within. Our family, other ranch families, the regular crew, all who stayed to see the season's harvest to the end, clustered around the cookhouse porch. Waiting. The bunkhouse gang, hatless, hair watered down, slicked back, scrubbed raw and shaved, scoured clean of harvest, their exciting banter blending to a hum. Waiting. Waiting for the clanging bell, the doors to open, waiting to fete the harvest.

It is a joyful bell that peals from the rooftop belfry, swings and clangs. At the summons the crowd inches forward, excited, swells toward the dining hall doors. Inside, the hall steams with a host of odors. We seat ourselves at tables laden with platters heaped with turkey, tubs of mashed potatoes, dressing, gravy boats that bubble and slosh, baskets of hot rolls heaped to precarious heights, bowls of smoking vegetables, fresh cider. It is a feast fit for a painter, a Rockwellian scene, Americana brought to table, seasoned with the salt of the earth.

Thus begins the Crane Ranch traditional harvest dinner. Both symbol and reward for a season of hard work, Crane & Crane foots the bill for the feast, is hosted by Francis G. himself, who now heads the head table. The din subsides as the men fall to, attack their brimming plates with the same determination and enthusiasm they brought to harvest. We eat and eat, pausing only to acknowledge a request to pass a plate or swipe away a dribble of wayward gravy with our napkins.

Halfway through the dessert course—the crew consumes wedge after wedge of pie (pumpkin lathered in whipped cream— and, of course, apple)—Francis sets his plate aside and stands. He waits to be recognized, for the chatter to trickle down; he is now master of the evening's ceremonies. A thanks to the crew for their hard work and dedication to the crop, for the tenacity to see the job through. A job well done. We applaud ourselves. As the crowd fusses and picks at their plates, Francis presents the awards: the women of the packing shed for tightest pack, best daily average pack out, are given envelopes. And applause. The men for most boxes picked, hours worked, receive envelopes, bonuses. And more applause.

The highlight of the evening Francis saves till last. Each year as the season progressed, the crew anted up a few dollars to wager on the crop's final pack out, the sum total of the season's packed fruit. (Even Dad faithfully took part every year, though to my knowledge he never won.) The harvest pool, the ranch lottery. Now Francis would reveal this year's winner. He always postponed the evening pronouncement by citing numbers, statistics, previous winners, comparisons to years past, anything to whet the suspense of the evening. After the hall was fraught with anxiety, Francis announced the winner, who amid hearty applause, came forward to claim the prize and proceeds, and the evening was officially over.

The next day the cookhouse doors would close. Within the week many of the crew, the migrant families, would leave the ranch, some to their homes in Arkansas, Alabama, Missouri, others to the flophouses in Portland or warmer climates further south. There they would winter, spend down their season's earnings until their return next spring or harvest.

But now there was a sense of closure, the year shut down, dormant like the orchard around us. Tonight we wandered home, feast-sated, beneath a different moon, a severe moon, harshly silver, not last month's orange, swollen orb, pregnant with harvest. A nimbus of frost encircled this moon, precursor of colder moons to follow, the moons of winter.

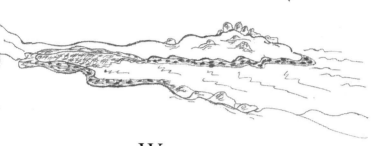

WINTER

Snowflakes, soft, gray bunnytails tumble down the sky. A thistledown blizzard they crowd and jostle each other to the ground. Billygoat is locked in a closet of snow. The gray water licks the rocks, and blacklipped, the island settles into winter. The flakes fall thick and heavy one upon the other, touch at last, and wrap the world in silence.

Where the hoarfrost filagrees the willows and the Old Dead Tree, the sun crusts with diamonds. A cobalt sky lies upon the river. Dervishes of steam whirl and twist themselves into oblivion, reappear, disappear. The island, margins trimmed in ice, its spine heavy with meringue, breaks the plane of the river like a giant white thumb. A kaleidoscope of feathers, a pheasant rooster struts his rainbow pride to the edge of the ice sheeting the island lagoon until it no longer supports his dignity. The ice gives way and in raucous indignation, the cock glides off into the shimmering day.

Christmas

But, thinkin' of the things yer'd like to see upon
that tree, Jest 'fore Christmas be as good as yer kin be.

Eugene Fields

Most of the year Tim, Kevin, Claudia, and I delighted in baiting, tormenting, banging one and the other about and wishing each were dead. Claudia and I would do battle at the kitchen sink after dinners (because we were the oldest, the chore fell to us), washing and drying the evening dishes, slinging suds, brandishing silverware, threatening each other with pots and pans (and once, I recall, a cast iron skillet with which to scramble egg one another's brains). Tim and Kevin were worrisome meddlers, always tattling, underfoot a thousand times a day in a thousand ways. To Mom and Dad surely we were a contentious brood. As I look back on those Christmases on the river, it's a wonder they didn't throw out the whole of Christmas and us along with it.

However, each Christmas Eve brought an uneasy truce to the home front. Perhaps because at this time of the year the Christmas spirit mandate coerced us to think of the other, not our selfish selves. The sense of wanting to please my brothers and sisters, gift them with some crudely wrapped package showed maybe I wasn't serious about wanting them dead after all. (Once I dug deep into my piggy bank, nearly bankrupted it, to buy my sister a twirling baton of twisted silver).

It was in the spirit of brotherly (and sisterly) love we huddled close in the stairwell on Christmas morning. Yes, whereas any other time of the year if one of us invaded the other's space, there was the sharp elbow, the vicious shove, the kicked shin, now we huddled against the cold and tingle of each other's excitement. Oh, how we loved Christmas. And the baby Jesus. And Mom and Dad. How my brothers and sisters loved me. And how I did love them. Sibling love so filled that dark stairwell where we sat, pajama-clad, bony little bottoms butted one against the other on those hardwood stairs, so much love that only a miracle kept the closed door below from bursting open with anticipation.

Yes, the anticipation. The stairwell door, I'm sure, Mom and Dad shut after we went to bed so Santa could work at will, do his magic while we slept. But, oh, what a pleasant barrier that door was. There could be anything and everything on the other side (though our loot never seemed to match the Cranes' who would later parade their plunder to our front door for show and tell).

After it seemed we had huddled for hours, one of us would venture an uncertain, "Can we come out yet?" (testing to see if Mom and Dad were up).

"Not yet!" (Yeea—they're up! Yeah! Ok!)

Then at intervals we repeated our plea: "Is it time yet?" Two or three minutes later: "Now is it time?"

"No, not quite yet!" and again we would squirm on those narrow wooden stairs. Then a hearty "Merry Christmas," our *Open Sesame* to the Christmas scene, signaled an end to our stairwell vigil. And the door would swing open to Christmas, and the glory corner where stood our tree of lights, our dreams heaped at its feet, mystery boxed and swaddled in ribbon and trappings. Our eyes darted from the angel atop the tree to the treasures she guarded from on high. Then next to the fireplace and the mantel where the thick knit red and green stockings hung, stuffed with what looked in all appearances to be elbows and knobby knees. (When we grew older, when we understood the Santa thing, two more stockings, one apiece for Mom and Dad, swung from our side of the door, Santa's validation that not only were there GOOD children in the household, but also GOOD parents.)

And what prizes would the stockings hold? Trinkets and knickknacks, thoughtful and personalized, bananas, oranges, a can of olives, always olives. On to the presents, which we opened one at a time as if we were on stage, a solo performance, Dad, with his Argus 35, recording each scene with a smoking flashbulb. The four of us had one BIG present each, the **Santa** present. The **Santa** presents I remember: a pair of glistening, powder-blue skis (they looked brilliant: two slices of sky hissing and skimming through the snow), a sled (though it wasn't a Flexible Flier but still gave your heart flip-flops on the riverbank sled run below the house), a pair of figure skates (for a boy?). Never once a BB gun (Dad had talked to an ophthalmologist); I finally gave up hope. A kit to make your very own radio, which I did and would listen to in bed late at night, and though I stretched seventy-five feet of antenna wire from my window to the nearest telephone pole, could never tune in a local station. But occasionally when I twisted the tuning coil, received a signal from some big kilowatt station out of California, usually Hispanic voices, a marvel to me—strange voices all the way from California to my bedside through my homemade radio.

So went a typical Christmas at the house on the river, the only time of the year our internecine warfare took a time out, a tacit truce. It never lasted, of course; two weeks, days (the very next, no doubt) later, our filial fractiousness resumed; again we were at each other's throats and shins and ribs. But for those precious few hours we thought only about the miracle of Christmas and presents and joy and love and each other.

The Five S's of Winter

Billygoat Mountain measured the descent of winter on our valley. Rising above the bend in the river at Pateros, Billygoat loomed against the western sky. I'm not sure how the mountain came by its name; we always referred to it as Billygoat or simply "The Goat." A mountain only in the sense it towered over the foothills and valley, the Goat was steeply rugged and sparsely forested with pine and fir where the trees could get a purchase on the craggy inclines. Certainly the Goat's terrain suited mountain goats, and though I often scanned the higher slopes and rock slides from the shores of Alta Lake, I never spotted one.

S is for Snow

Snow is not silent
Down the fir's needles it sings
A soft, crystal song.

It is hard to know which delights children more: snow or the anticipation of it. When the mid November storms cruised in from the west, we would watch for the first tell-tale gauzy fingers of cloud to settle upon the topmost crags of the Goat. We were snow experts and could readily distinguish snow clouds from rain. "It's snowing on the Goat" signaled the onset of winter. Week by week the snow level crept lower, dusting the flanks of the mountain, and one morning we would awaken to a world of white.

I do not recall many severe winters while we lived on the river. One winter came and went nearly snowless. Oldtimers, however, remembered winters when snow covered the fence posts: you could ski across fence lines. Also, I heard stories about the river channel entirely locked in ice (most likely before dams choked the river), allowing skaters to skim the seven miles of river from Pateros to Brewster, in company with horse drawn sleighs which glided among them along the frozen channel. I remember one early winter when ten inches of snow cancelled school the day before Thanksgiving. It was a day of double delights. We strapped on our skis, had a rigorous Nordic outing and then schussed home where we put our napkins on our lapkins and bellied up to the turkey.

...And Sleds

Winter meant adventures sledding, skiing, and skating. My earliest memories of winter sports involved crude carpentry and homemade toboggans. These we cobbled together from the pine slats of apple box sides: two for the sliding surface, one on top for a seat, which we nailed across the lower seam to connect the two. All seams we overlaid with the sides of coffee cans, hammered flat and tacked down. Half an apple box side served as the prow of our snow toys, toenailed to the sliding surface at a forty-five degree angle, the seam also covered with Folgers tin. To grease our daring descents, we liberally applied to the sliding surface any paraffin sealing wax or candle butts we could lay our hands on.

The prototype apple box toboggan was the brainchild of my friend Mervyn Gragg whose fertile mind knew no boundaries, be it food preparation (a secret blend of kitchen oils and spices, strong to Worchestershire and garlic, brewed, bottled, stoppered, and labeled *Cure-All*) or electronics (his bedroom a jumble of parted out radios, TVs, boxes of circuit boards, colorful resistors...). On these crude pine vehicles we would carom down the steep hillsides above the orchard, skidding wildly, our direction chiefly determined by the contours of the snow, until we reached the bottom of the slope, or more the case, have our run aborted by a large sagebrush. This common occurrence usually broke the prow or doubled it back, disabling the sled, and sending us to the shop for repairs. We would plod back up to the head of the run for another downhill rush, towing our toboggans behind us on a tether of bailing twine. We quickly learned our toboggans would function on crusted snow only; in fresh snow we would plunk ourselves down at the top of the hill where we immediately sank into the powder, stuck fast, wishing for the wind in our faces, the bottom of the slope mocking us below.

My hands were ill-suited for saw and hammer, my constitution shy on patience, so constructing a toboggan was a frustrating ordeal. Often as not, when I lifted my sled, the prow flopped and dangled, attached only by the tin can splice; the nails had all pulled loose. This fore-section of the sled was crucial, for it plowed aside the snow, allowed the sled to coast forward. Without the prow, the sled would auger in beneath the snow, preventing further forward progress. Without the prow, no matter how you distributed your weight, you always grounded out. By this stage of the project, I was usually reduced to angry tears.

The coasting sled, a less novel but considerably more efficient vehicle, was more to my liking. Constructed by real craftsmen, our sleds had sturdy steel runners and hardwood slats for the riding surface, built for rugged use and to rugged use we put them. Aptly named "Flexible Fliers" these stout coasters gave us hours of downhill entertainment and exercise, whenever and wherever the geography declined.

We designed a coasting hill that traversed our upper and lower lawns to the bank below. At the Old Dead Tree the run banked hard left and continued riverward through a cut lined by willows and snakeweed where we burst out onto the river cobbles in a shower of sparks. One day I made the initial run, and as I jetted through the cut, was astonished to see the outrun under water. The river level had risen during the night. I bailed into a snow bank and the sled skidded on without me, splashing to rest in the river ten feet from the amended shore. Thereafter we always scouted the run before we took to our sleds.

We boarded our sleds using one of two methods. Stylistically, coasting prone was the safer, less daring of the two. Each hand on the steering arms, down you went, low to the ground, your center of gravity usually making for a safe run; if your speed exceeded your comfort zone, you slowed by dragging your galoshes. Shifting your legs left or right and dragging your feet helped you negotiate the challenging turns. Coasting prone, the hazards were few, although you cruised along with your face close to the action and the business end of the sled. Ice crystals flung up by the runners would sting your face. On bitter cold days, you were careful to keep your tongue clear of the steering harness unless you wanted to tow the sled upslope attached to it.

For the extreme sledding experience you assumed the upright, sitting position. Then grasping a rear runner arch in each hand, you secured both feet on the steering arms and had a playmate give you a running shove and commit you to your fate. Then you were committed to speed, having no way to slow your downhill rush (in desperation you might extend your feet, stiff-legged, in a bone jarring effort to control your momentum but most likely were tumbled end over end for your troubles). Downhill you plunged, truly a part of the sledding experience. The upright position raised your center of gravity, increasing the risk of being flipped over or thrown from the sled. Hit a bump and one foot— or both—might jolt from the steering arms, and there you were helter skelter on the course, out of control, heading for the next turn or disaster. The more daring usually "sat" the course, although extreme icy conditions ultimately dictated our sledding strategy. Of course, sledding tandem brought even more variety to the coasting experience.

I thought our sledding episodes worthy enough to record on film and during one stint, armed with my little box camera, I attempted some action photography. I stationed myself at a challenging leg of the run and snapped a twelve print roll of black and white film. In a shoebox somewhere in an old photo Tim hangs suspended above a bump, the next turn imminent, mouth grim between two cold flushed cheeks, as intent as any luge rider contending for the gold. Though the photo was black and white, I swear you can see Tim's cheeks aglow with excitement and concentration, two ruddy apples set either side of his mouth.

...And Skis

Luck brought us skis one Christmas. Mine were powderblue, beautiful as the eyes of a Nordic lass. No prettier slats ever existed. I can still hear the hiss they made on plane, the blue tips slicing aside the white powder with each downhill plunge, my ski poles windmilling at my sides as I tried to keep up with the boards strapped to my feet. Unlike our sleds, which in deep snow were useless except as a place to sit, skis gave us the run of the countryside; wherever the snow lay deep enough to cover the rocks, we ventured. We were mostly downhill skiers; our skill required an obstacle-free run or snow deep enough to cover potential obstructions. Though our runs were free of tree hazards, we often had to negotiate the occasional sagebrush or greasewood. On one such course my left ski speared a sagebrush looped just above the snow, causing that side of me to stop abruptly one moment and then both sides to tumble in a whirl of skis and poles. I came to rest with a badly sprained but colorful thumb. Much to my disgust, (except when I chose to share my injury with my classmates) this digit oozed green stuff from beneath the thumbnail for days.

I suppose we could have become fairly competent skiers had we the luxury of tows or lifts to shorten the return trip and allow more time to practice turns and slaloms in the downhill phase of the sport. Our skiing experience, however, amounted mostly to the uphill phase; we were nearly always trudging upslope for the reward of a few more seconds of wind in our faces.

For some reason skiing enticed us to go air born. Perhaps the annual ski jumping contests at Leavenworth inspired our aerial pursuits. When we lived in Wenatchee our family attended at least one of these competitions. I watched in astonishment as stocking capped Torgersons, Jahrlbergs, and Svensons, speeding dots, darted down the steep run and hurled themselves into space from the lip of the jump, soared gracefully yards (or meters, for they used the metric system) down the landing slope where they touched down— sometimes not so gracefully, and skidded to a stop amid cheers and applause. (I remember that day well because Mom served us steaming home made clam chowder from a squat silver thermos).

This kind of romance we wished to duplicate in our own skiing experience. At the steepest incline of our run, we would shovel a mound of snow and pack it with our skis, shovel on more to increase the height and pack it hard again. If we were lucky, a warming trend and rain would compress the jump more, making it concrete firm when the temperatures dipped again. Once again we would heap on more snow, hoping to increase the height of this icy sculpture. And then we wanna-be Torgersons, Jahrlbergs, and Svensons plodded to the head of the run to begin our contest.

Whereas our Nordic role models, who no doubt had spent the better part of their lives gliding on snow, worried only about take offs and stylish landings, we found it challenging enough just to hit the jump squarely. Inexperience frequently caused our skis to leave their parallel track, a distraction that led us to stray the course; sometimes we missed the jump altogether; sometimes only one ski found it. Having to take the high road and low simultaneously led to an assortment of desperate acrobatics that usually ended down slope in a tangle of limbs and skis. Sometimes the violence of the fall would jar loose a ski, which freed from a clumsy foot would clatter and careen downhill through the orchard, past the outrun, out of sight. Then amid execrations as strong as Sunday School training would allow, the unfortunate sportsman had to remove the remaining faithful ski and plod after its renegade partner while the rest of us did battle on the hill.

After continued use of the run, we wore ruts or grooves in the course, allowing us to hit the jump square most of the time, a kind of consistency that permitted us to pursue competition in earnest. One of us would sit out a round to serve as official judge, calculating the distance of the "leap" (in English measurement) by measuring the span between the base of the jump and the marks left as the skis touched down. After each run and subsequent measurement, the judge smoothed and prepared the landing site for the next jumper in much the same fashion as the broad jump event. Once the round was finished, the judge turned contestant for the next. In truth, this part of the contest served no purpose than to mimic the professional Nordic event, for try as we might, no matter how hard we hurled ourselves from the jump, we would return to find the distance of the leap equal to that of the length of our skis, the official measurement confirmed and pointed out by the judge: two parallel skid marks down the face of the jump. He with the longest skis, wins: we didn't soar from the jump, simply fell off the end. Perhaps some of the lightweights managed to put some distance between the foot of the jump and their landings, but I can't remember any flights worthy of "oohs" and "aahs"; certainly no leap of the heavyweights drew cheers. A moment of suspended silence, then a kerplop and depending on the landing, an erratic or uneventful schuss downhill, our "leaps" flights of fancy only.

We enjoyed ski touring too. In those days we were wheat field skiers. Strapping on our skis, we headed south off the county road uphill through the new orchard to the wheat fields east of Central Ferry Canyon. One trek I recall in particular because it was a day of stark contrast, a January day, I think, when the temperature was in the high teens, low twenties. A chilly ice fog clung to the valley (not one of those nostril-pinching bitter cold days when your water-slicked hair froze, and you arrived at the bus stop brittle coiffed, hair ice-shellacked). The snow lay deep and crusted. An inch of crystal rime, ice fog precipitate, dusted the surface. One by one apple trees loomed out of the gray like ghostly sentinels as we shuffled and herringboned our way south. Next, up the sagebrush slope, greasewood brush swirling in the fog. Suddenly, we broke over the crest of the hill into a bejeweled world, a landscape set aglitter by a sun that blazed from a sky so blue it shocked your eyes. We had entered an ice world: every bush, frond of grass, strand of barbed wire was encrusted by hoarfrost diamonds, a world of Thor and Freya, a Valhalla of rime and hoar. We paused, not to catch our breath (which steamed and smoked in the steely air), but because we were beauty-blinded. In disbelief we turned and looked back down trail, the way we had climbed. The valley was gone; the river, the ranch, the orchards below pressed into soft, gray oblivion by a crenulated comforter of fog. The pastor said, "Let us rejoice in this day that the Lord hath made." And it was on such a day we climbed the highest wheat field, our herringbone ascent faceting drift after diamond sprinkled drift behind us. Then the downward rush, the momentary bite of fear as speed contended with control. A few brief minutes and we had traversed the distance of a half day's journey. Downhill and home to a warm meal and bath. Later to sleep, to dream (perchance) of a kingdom of diamonds.

...And Skates

Below the cookhouse on the bank above the island sat an eight unit wooden frame bunkhouse. One fall, my seventh grade year, the bunkhouse burned completely down and Puddy One-Eye burned completely up. And that's how we became ice skaters. The charred debris was cleared; the cabin woodstoves and singed plumbing hauled away; all remnants removed from the site, which was bulldozed level. That winter, to involve the ranch children in yet another winter recreation, Francis Crane designated the site a skating rink.

As soon as night temperatures dropped to the low twenties or teens, the one hundred by thirty foot rectangle was flooded. Then the night work began. Francis assigned Billy Hogan, one of the ranch regulars, night shift, paying him salary to create a training rink on which to develop the Crane & Crane Ice Follies. Working by the light of a temporary flood lamp, Billy sprayed layer upon layer of water on the frozen surface, augmenting the frozen base. There was an art to rink building. Water had to be sprayed evenly on the new ice. If it puddled too deeply, air pockets formed; the ice became honeycombed and pocked. The resulting weak spot would collapse beneath a skater's weight, usually tripping him face forward on the ice. You had to work the spray slowly the length of the rink, return to the starting point, repeat the procedure. Rink building required cold night temperatures to create a smooth, hard surface—the faster the water froze, the more solid the base for each subsequent layer. Night after night Billy worked, late into dawn, bundled up like an Inuit, ice crystals swirling around the flood light, water hissing from the hose.

I remember the disappointment, looking at our indoor-outdoor thermometer and groaning with impatience when the column hovered around thirty: no Billy tonight, no more progress. Darn! I would have to wait another day before I could launch my skating career. Daily we would check the progress at the rink, wondering which would expire first: our patience or the winter. Then one bitter crisp day the ice lay thick and smooth, a sturdy gray, ready for the first pratfall.

That year the winter sports' section of every Sears & Roebuck and Montgomery Ward catalog ("Monkey Ward's," we called it) on the ranch was thumbed to a frazzle. Every kid—and some grownups (a pair of hockey skates for Dad)—unwrapped a pair of skates for Christmas. Toddlers opened shoeboxes and puzzled at the contents, strange pairs of shoes, each sprouting twin blades, the young skater's equivalent of training wheels. Gleaming blades and leather so shiny it mirrored the tree lights, gifts far superior to the traditional: the annual garment gamut from those adults who believed shirts, jeans, and undergarments to be, if not exotic, certainly practical gifts for children. These we opened perfunctorily, feigning delight, conditioned to show gratitude for any gift personally tagged with our names. All the while our thoughts were on those glorious skates and that virgin slab of ice just up the road.

Skating, we quickly discovered, allowed us to experience a wide range of emotions and sensations in a brief span of time—usually in antithesis of each other: exhilaration and frustration, joy and anger, laughter and tears, pleasure and pain, all stemming from the ups and downs of our efforts. For the first few minutes it seemed ice and steel repelled each other like the opposite poles of magnets. "Ice Follies" perhaps best spelled *fallies*) literally described our early antics on the ice: it was as if we were trying to negotiate a marble covered floor. One minute you were running in place; the next, you were on your back, gazing skyward at flailing feet and skates, or sprawled face down, staring cross-eyed at your reflection, counting tiny bubbles in the ice. You dared not laugh at each other's pratfalls—at least while you were upright. A smile's effort was sure to trip you up; a guffaw and you became a statistic. We learned, also, a certain kinesthetic came into play on the rink: closing to within a foot of a fellow bladesman often caused us both to spill spread eagled on the ice.

Two or three hours later we were skilled enough to navigate the length of the rink with a minimum of interruptions. Stopping was simple: just fall—or stumble—into the snow bank on each end. Now we had to tackle the corners. Here was a demanding challenge; deviating from the straight line—intentionally—required considerable risk taking. So we practiced the crossover step technique and soon the snow banks at the corners were pocked with snow angels, by-products of our cornering attempts. Because of the crossover maneuver, we frequently collided at the corners. Those of us who used the right over left technique circled the rink counterclockwise while the left-over righters rotated clockwise. On crowded days the corners were like a hockey rink—all players converging at once on the puck. To break the monotony of the circle routine, we had contests to see who could complete the most laps without taking a tumble. At the outset, our skating antics must have seemed like a flea circus on amphetamines to the curious bystander, but I must admit, after a few days of practice we showed promise, if not some finesse on the ice.

Philosophical differences existed between the hockey and figure skate camps. Those who had hockey skates considered themselves the more manly skaters: hockey, after all, was a rough and tumble sport, requiring stamina and a high pain threshold. Figure skates, on the other hand, were for girls, the dainties of the ice: these were usually cutesy, white leather with faux fur bordering the tops. For some strange reason the girls wove small bells into their laces, which seemed silly to me, although the tinkling sound made it easier to locate the young ladies in the dark. I experimented with both varieties and decided to chance sissyness by choosing figure skates. Mine were black leather. No feminine trappings for me. I liked that the blades of my skates were hollow ground, concave, two surfaces of blade to grab the ice. Also, three or four sharp teeth protruded from the tip of each runner. Once I learned to skate backwards, I found I could stop by standing slightly tiptoe, a maneuver that allowed the prongs to grab the ice. Then as an impressive shower of ice sprayed from each toe, you came to an abrupt stop. With figure skates an adept skater could execute a variety of moves, spins—and figures—with fluid grace (though I practiced several moves repeatedly, my repertoire of the spectacular consisted of only my abrupt stops). With hockey skates one had speed and mobility but lacked the tools for cutting fancy didoes in the ice. I had a friend who owned a pair of speed skates, skates with blades two feet long, which sailed you down the ice with giant strides. Meant for great expanses of ice, his skates were useless on our small rink, a Ferrari in city traffic, the long runners more a hazard than anything else, like skating on machetes.

A rink full of amateurs was tough on the skating surface. Two days' use and the ice was scarred, gouged, and chipped so that some areas of the rink were a hazard to navigate. After Billy finished the rink, Francis G. gave over its maintenance to the skaters. I spent some late nights myself on the end of the spray hose, layering on more ice, smoothing the surface, an adolescent Zamboni spraying away in the night's sub zero cold.

Usually a day with brilliant, cloudless skies forecasted a night of zero to sub zero cold. On these nights we resurfaced the rink. (After dinner on such nights under a wreathing Milky Way I would tag along with Dad on his routine checks of the cold storage shed where he monitored temperatures among the tiers of packed boxes, making sure the fruit did not freeze. I was always pleasantly surprised when the heavy doors clacked shut the bitter chill behind us and we entered the "warmth" of the huge rooms where the temperature hovered just above freezing.) When such a resurfacing session was imminent, our last task of the day was to sweep the ice free of chunks and chips of ice that would otherwise cement themselves to the skating surface during the surfacing. With push brooms in hand two or three of us would work the length of the rink, back and forth, careful not to chip up more chunks with our skates, until we had swept the surface clean. Then off with the skates: no more skating until the night's work was behind us.

A snowstorm required more maintenance: you couldn't skate on a rink you couldn't see, and besides, the snow made each skate a snowplow, quickly clogged your skates. We would have to clear the rink before skating resumed. Accumulations of soft powder of an inch or less we removed much the same way we prepared the ice for resurfacing: up and down the rink with the brooms, pushing the snow before us. I remember, however, one heavy snowfall where shovels were required to clear the rink, a task that took us several hours to complete. Shovel, take a step, throw the snow to one side, until we removed enough of the stuff to resume our push broom procedure. Though snow removal consumed valuable skating time, there were advantages: the heaping piles provided more rink side cushioning, a softer landing pad, for we still took the occasional header. We performed these tasks without grousing–and gladly. After all, it was **our** skating rink.

The rink became a gathering place for ranch society that winter. To thank Francis and our parents for a new recreational opportunity, we decided to stage a show on ice, a Crane & Crane kids' ice gala, a skating spectacular. For the better part of Christmas vacation we practiced, choreographed routines, fine tuned our moves. The show starred every kid in camp: the Johnson kids, Mike and Wayland Lowrance, the lovely and graceful White sisters, Lynn, Nadine, Phyllis, and Connie, and older brother Jimmy. The Crane kids rounded out our cast of skaters. The rehearsals were long and intense, for our standards would allow nothing less than precision and perfection.

The show lasted about an hour. Our parents, dragged duty-bound from cozy hearths, stood knee deep in snow and watched patiently as we executed our routines. With smiles of appreciation literally frozen on their faces, they watched us navigate, circumnavigate the rink countless times. We skated in pairs, by threes, arms linked; we cornered; we negotiated the ice forward, then backward. We skated clockwise. We skated counterclockwise. Hands on the hips of the preceding skater, we formed a human chain and made two or three circuits clinging desperately to each other, like some convoluted ice worm about to cast off body segments. In retrospect, I believe that hour must have seemed interminable to the parents, the cold exacerbated by our tedious antics. ("Spending quality time with the children," today's term for our parents' participation.) The only break in our circuitous monotony was when a performer took a sudden unrehearsed header or pratfall. Fortunately enough of these occurred to sustain our doting, but hypothermic audience, who obviously were thankful for the comedy, and did their best to stifle their laughter.

I remember hosting few parties growing up on the river those years, but one occurred that winter. During my seventh grade year, I had invested my affections in a young lady, Miss Lynne Hymer, one of my seventh grade classmates. Young Lynne had that special feminine mystique seventh grade boys looked for in a woman, and she was a much sought after prize. And thus I was not the only suitor who vied for her attention. At lunch time Dean Heidi plied Lynne with ice cream sandwiches, trying to buy her love. In attempt to win her heart, I believe Dean's dessert designs bankrupted him. He squandered his lunch money for the year, and perhaps the next, for Dean's education ended with the seventh grade; he never returned to the eighth grade and the competition for Lynne's affections was trimmed by one.

Other boys used their prowess on the basketball court to impress Lynne. I badly needed an edge because I was too cheap to buy a girl's love and too thin skinned to tolerate a coach's yelling and criticism on the court. But I was the only seventh grade boy with a skating rink practically in his backyard, and I was quick to use this commodity to leverage my position and gain the upper hand in the competition. I had heard a rumor to the effect that Lynne "liked me," (a vicious rumor, no doubt), and in a moment of weakness, shared this information with Mom. To foster our "friendship," she suggested I host a skating party, invite Lynne and a few other friends. We set a date; I passed out the invitations, and my friends came, Lynne among them. The skating rink worked its special magic that night. Though Ron Pasley, my fiercest competitor in the crusade for Lynne's heart, was among my guests, it was I who held her hand as the party goers trudged to the rink through the snowy night. It was I who helped her to her feet after each fall–and they were numerous, as she was new to the sport. Ron, who had as much down time as Lynne, was too occupied picking his own self off the ice to interfere with my overtures. It was I who squeezed her hand in the dark on the return trip. And whose hands were on Lynne's hips when Mom taught us the "Bunny Hop" later that evening? I made sure they were mine.

But love is one of life's ephemera, especially to a smitten seventh-grader. Unfortunately, the ice melted before the basketball season ended. The romance of the court ended ours of the rink, and Lynne's affections shifted to some forward, guard, or center, leaving my heart permanently benched, to watch the game of love from the sidelines of disappointment. For one night, however, with my gleaming skates and that magical sheet of ice, I came so close to skating my way into Lynne Hymer's heart.

Once you learn the art, skating, like swimming, is one you never forget, and though I can remember the ranch skating rink a one year affair only, we had other skating opportunities. We employed our skates and skills wherever we found a frozen pond that would support our weight and was large enough to allow a variety of movement. The winters the lake down Dougherty Canyon froze over, we would hike there and skate. If enough kids were up to the hike, we teamed up and played hockey. None of us owned regulation equipment, so we scoured the banks and improvised. Branches from downed serviceberry bushes or cherry birch made dandy hockey sticks. Because the range cattle watered at the pond, we had little trouble finding a puck, or more appropriately, a "puckey." I recall several spirited games of ice puckey down the canyon. The speed with which those permafrosted meadow muffins skimmed the ice when given a good lick was truly amazing.

Because of the lengthy hike to the lake, we did not skate Dougherty often. We were usually tired when we arrived, and after an hour or two of exercise on the lake it was all we could do to drag ourselves home, a long trip made even longer when you were a tired and cold skater.

Good skiing winters usually meant poor ones for skating. Small accumulations of wet snow froze to the ice and crusted there, creating a surface that made skating poor at best. Dry, powdery snow the wind would sometimes clear for us, but snowless winters were the best for skating. And whenever we had one of these (I can remember two such in the ten years I lived on the river), we loaded our skates in the car and headed for Alta Lake.

Skating Alta was great fun. You could skate a full mile the length of the lake, or if you wanted a greater distance, you could circumnavigate its shores. One bitter winter the ice froze several inches thick. Later a winter storm covered the ice with nearly a foot of snow, but no matter: a local orchardist brought a tractor equipped with a push blade, drove onto the ice, and in three or four hours cleared several hundred yards of snow, and we took to the ice again.

At Alta, the best skating I remember was one of those snowless winters. The ice froze thick and clear. When you skated the shores, you could see the lake bottom in the shallows. If you were lucky, you might see a turtle or a trout swimming along beneath your skates. I marveled that a wooden buoy I swam to or rowed by in the summer now provided me a place to sit and tighten my skate laces. On the east end of the lake along the rock slide, huge boulders loomed mossy from the depths. This side of the lake you skated with caution: springs trickling from the rock slide warmed the water there and thinned the ice. I gave the springs a wide berth when I skirted the rock slide. Where you skated over great depths, the ice lay thick and black.

I loved the freedom of the open ice. You skimmed the surface with great sliding strides. With the thrust of each blade, a hollow, pinging sound reverberated from the ice. I imagined myself on the great canals of Holland and cruised the ice Hans Brinker style, hands clasped behind my back. Stroke, glide and sway, covering great distances quickly and with ease. To assume the classic skater's look, you wore a long scarf, which trailed in your slipstream, a visual tribute to speed.

Ice acts like a living thing: it moves, expands, contracts. That bitter cold winter it boomed and cracked, created fissures hundreds of feet long, froze solid again–apparently. These cracks gave me pause. I was afraid they would open again, cutting me off a quarter mile from shore. Or they would suddenly open between my legs and swallow me up. When I skated Alta, I always carried two large spikes on the chance if the ice betrayed me, I could use them as picks and pull myself from the water to safety.

When the sun dropped in the west, an avalanche of cold slid down the Goat, pressed heavily on the lake. Then the ice boomed and rumbled. Once when I was mid lake, the ice thundered. Terrified, I rode an adrenalin rush, skimming the ice with gargantuan strides to shore, expecting any moment to be floundering amid ice floes, struggling in the frigid, black waters of the lake.

But I suffered only one misadventure on the ice that year. In sub zero temperatures I made a crosslake run at twilight. The cold stung my cheeks. With each intake of bitter air, my nostrils pinched shut. The billowing scarf failed to protect my ears, and by the time I returned to shore, both were numb with frostbite. The next day they erupted in huge water blisters, sagged from the weight, and hung down just like in the song (you know the lyrics: "Do your ears hang low, do they wobble to and fro…"). The blisters broke and oozed sticky stuff for the next few days. And then at school, as if my ears were snakes at shedding time, I peeled fillets of dead skin from them, which I then arranged in piles on my desk in full view for my classmates, who were repulsed (as was my intent) to queasiness.

Common sense breeds prudence and at my age I had very little of both. If I had possessed more of either, I would have tugged a wool cap tightly over my ears before pitting my proud flesh against the chill factor. And because I lacked these qualities, one winter I set out on an adventure that turned dark and ugly, an adventure where I thought my doom imminent, where I came close to freezing to death.

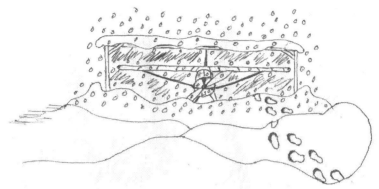

...And for Scared

I was a Boy Scout in those days and fourteen years old. The scouting motto "Be Prepared" had been drummed into us scouts since our tenderfoot days, but like everything else in my life, then, I took scouting lightly. The motto was good enough in theory, but that winter day I was definitely not prepared for what happened later.

To hone our winter wood lore skills, we hardy scouts would organize an occasional hike and cookout. We would march a mile or two into the woods on Paradise Hill, hunt up some squaw wood and pitch drippings, build a "one match" fire, cook up a hearty wilderness stew, and hike back to civilization. The romance of a big pot of stew bubbling away over a crackling fire in a snowbound wilderness inspired me to try my own cookout–solo. Another tenet of scouting advises the buddy system: "buddy up" with a partner before venturing into the woods. But that day I ignored this principle as well, set it aside along with "Be Prepared," packed my camp kit and ingredients for my woodsman's stew in my day pack, and late morning, ventured forth.

The snowfall had been considerable that winter; off the beaten path the snow measured mid-thigh, lay crusted, though not enough to bear my weight. Hiking in those conditions was difficult and tiring. With each step you had to punch your foot through the crust, and then you were thigh deep again. You trudged along, punching a hole a step at a time, advancing slowly like climbing a hill, while all the time on the level. I knew I could avoid much of this troublesome terrain if I slogged down to the river where the water had receded and proceed over the bare rock unencumbered by the crusted drifts. I plodded down the cut in the bank where the pump house sat dormant on its rails and skirting the owl thicket east of the cut, headed along the bank up the river bar.

The fact my outing had begun amid a light snowfall only added to the adventure: I would really be "roughing it" it now. Though the footing was tricky because of the scum-covered rocks, I was able to make good time. A half hour later I had covered more than a quarter mile of riverbank, enough terrain to achieve just the proper wilderness for a campfire and an outdoorsman's hearty meal.

When I had begun the hike, the hills across the river were still visible through the gentle sift of snow. Now the flakes fell thicker, more determined; I could barely spy the opposite bank through the spiraling flakes. Turning my back to the river, I headed toward the willow thickets below Chapman's peach orchard. The thickets would be my cookout site, a sheltered spot where I could find fuel for a fire. To reach the thickets I had to traverse the barren river bank and break trail through two hundred yards of knee deep, crusted snow.

In the swale below the orchard I chose a suitable campfire site, kicked aside the snow to clear a fire pit and began gathering fuel from the dead willows in the thicket. By the time I had my small cook fire crackling and laid aside a surplus of branches and twigs, it was early afternoon. I unpacked my tin kettle and stuffed it brimful with snow: melt water for my stew. I jammed a sturdy branch into the snow and from it dangled the kettle over the fire. The snow melted quickly. Into the kettle I threw the vegetables and stew meat I had prepared in a warm kitchen earlier that day and waited for the fire to do its job.

If I had not been so preoccupied, I would have noticed the snow had thickened, the river now visible only as a faint, black trace through the gray, tumbling snow. Since I could find only twigs and small branches, none larger than an inch and a half in diameter, the willow fuel burned quickly. My forays for fuel took me in widening circles beyond the fire. I noticed an additional two or three inches of fresh snow now covered the crusted base. Though my cook fire was too small to radiate much heat, it was cheerful enough, and I was glad to return to fireside and tend the meal in progress.

The snow cascaded down. Large, thick flakes jostled each other in a crowded sky: the hills, the river–even the nearby willow thickets–all consumed by a sky heavy with snow and the dwindling light of a short winter's day. As I studied the surface of the kettle, waiting for the first bubbles to rise in a boil, I became conscious of a lowering gloom, an eerie silence; that home was a good distance away; that my feet were leaden with cold; that I was very, very alone. The exercise of gathering fuel had kept my feet somewhat warm, but now as I stood waiting for the pot to boil, I was aware they were numbed senseless. What heat the fire provided was concentrated on the stew pot, and as the storm closed in around me, the warmth seemed subdued by the endless barrage of falling snow. I watched the pot anxiously.

I think I know at what point adventure turned to ordeal, romance to fear. Sometimes I would ride the school bus an additional mile to Dennis Gragg's house where we played indoor basketball (for a basket we used a round oatmeal carton nailed above the doorway, shot a tinfoil ball to score). Afterwards I would walk the long mile home alone in the dark. Many a night I took that walk, scuffling along the dusty county road, unafraid (though I might cast a suspicious glance at an unfamiliar shape or configuration lurking in the brush off road). When I reached the end of our driveway, however, and saw our porch light, a cheery, bare bulb lighting the front porch, I experienced the feeling that something was behind me. In near terror I would break into a dead run, head full tilt for the savior light, open the door and rush breathless into the house.

This strange thing happened time and time again (I was always too terrified to look over my shoulder and put to rest once and for all my irrational fear that some fiendish monster was fast bearing down upon me).

Now as I stood on club-like feet by a dwindling fire in the swirling snow and fading light, I thought about home: the warm kitchen, the fireplace and blazing apple logs, the sentinel porch-light—and I panicked.

The kettle had hardly begun to bubble when I snatched the handle and dumped the steaming contents into the fire. I did not even have the presence of mind to eat the stew: at least I would have had my last supper. I snatched up a mitten of snow, quickly swabbed out the kettle and jammed it into my pack. Turning my back on the smoldering fire, I set out for the river through a twilight laden with snow, retracing my trail to the bank. I did not know it then, but I was about to begin a fearful ordeal.

It was my plan, once I reached the river, to return home along the bank the way I had come, making much better time over the slippery rocks than floundering through the snowdrifts. I was not prepared for what I found when I reached the bank. In the short two hours I was occupied with my cookout activities, the river had risen (because of Chief Joseph Dam, these fluctuations were common during the winter months; the river would drop overnight, then rise again during the day). My path along the river was now submerged, the water nearly up to the snow rimmed bank. Scarcely a foot of bare shore remained. In horror I looked at the slippery trace where the water rushed by deep and black and knew to negotiate that narrow path was to court certain disaster. One slip and the river would snatch me up and sweep me away where I would be sucked to the bottom, pulled down by the weight of my winter clothing and snow boots. My only option, I reasoned, was to return to the willows and continue homeward though the crusted snow, though I knew to cross the snow laden river bar would prove the longer distance. At least I had a partially broken trail to the willows. Fighting back panic, I set out.

Though visibility was perhaps only twenty feet in any direction, I was never in any danger of being lost. During hunting season I had combed every inch of this riverbank with a dog and shotgun countless times and knew exactly where I was. But this was the problem: I knew how much snow-covered terrain lay between me and home. By this time I was beginning to lose feeling in my fingers as well. I passed through the willows, past the dead fire and, smacking my mittens together to drive the numbness from my fingers, I left the willow coverts behind in the falling snow. A low bank separated the swales of willow from Chapman's peach orchard. I slogged up the bank and into the orchard where the trees stood bare and stark against the snow. I knew beyond the peach orchard was an access road. My hopes lifted. Perhaps the going would be easier on the road. I chose the closest two rows and plodded along between them.

I staggered from the orchard into the road. No relief there. The road had not been plowed: the snow lay there just as deep. I would have to continue as before, one slow step after the other, on feet like clubs, on toes that had no feeling. Just as I was about to turn right and follow the invisible track that led to another and then yet another before I reached safety, through the silent snow, a shape, a structure of some kind loomed from the barren field. This fifty acre field had yet to be planted in orchard and now served as a landing strip for Mel Chapman's small airplane. The lurking shape was the hangar Mel had built for his plane, now snowbound until spring. I thought immediately of shelter, some cover, a respite from the interminable snow, a chance, even to warm myself and labored toward the hangar.

Though open to the weather on three sides, the hangar floor was bare. What a relief to walk on bare ground, albeit on legs of rubber, and not have to force your way forward every step you took. Outside the hangar the snow fell relentlessly. I stepped to the plane, opened the passenger door, and crawled inside the cramped two passenger cabin. Some canvas rags lay behind the seats, and I quickly swaddled my senseless feet in these. I removed my mittens and tucked my tingling fingers beneath my coat, digging for warmth. I curled up, knees to chin, and tried to worm my way deeper into my clothing, curling up like a distressed sow bug.

The cabin was cold as a tomb. I huddled inside for fifteen, maybe twenty minutes. No warmth returned, only panic and fear. If I stayed much longer, I thought, come spring Mel would find the body of a hapless Boy Scout, who unprepared, had gambled with the elements and lost, his passenger a teenage corpse. Out there in the snow and surrounding darkness, home seemed distant, irretrievable. My only chance was to keep moving. In desperation I forced my shivering body out of the plane, beyond the hangar and into the storm.

The last expanse of drifted terrain between me and home was the pear orchard. When the first row of barren trees appeared through the curtain of snow, I found new resolve; perhaps I would survive after all. I trudged doggedly up the snowbound access road to begin my final assault on home. Resolve soon turned to blessed relief: to my surprise I found the service road had been plowed so the workers could access the orchard for its annual pruning. For the last leg of the journey I could use both of mine to full advantage. To this day I remain firm in my belief that Providence in the form of a plowed road saved my life. And just as darkness shut the day, I saw the lights of home.

My homecoming was anticlimactic. The family, unaware of my snow flurried ordeal, listened to my tale of survival with mild interest now that I was safely home. Aside from the tingling and burning of feet and fingers as the circulation returned to these extremities, I remember only one other consequence from my winter's adventure. Days later Mel Chapman confronted Dad, wanted to know who had broken into his plane and rifled its contents. In my efforts to warm myself, I had apparently left the cabin in disarray. I believe I may have abandoned my daypack intentionally, my attempt to leave behind any encumbrances that might hinder my flight to safety. Mel Chapman was not a patient man, and though Dad explained my fear and desperation in an attempt to placate him, there followed recriminations and threats to notify and involve the sheriff. I believe I was required to offer various apologies, either written or face-to-face, and tidy up the plane. How the incident played out is hazy; I do recall it took several days for me to find the courage to return to "the scene of the crime" and retrieve my gear.

After a long, warm soak in the tub, one spent Boy Scout went to bed early that night. I crawled into bed beneath thick blankets. I burrowed into their warmth. Instantly an avalanche of sleep crashed down. And in my sleep I dreamt my legs would not stop moving. They churned away through drifts of snow, churning on through the winter, churning on and on into spring.

SPRING

When the world is puddle wonderful...

e.e. cummings

Spring does not announce itself. Stealthily it creeps around the coattails of winter, comes whistling up the river in disguise, flings whitecap spittle against the island, swirls and eddies through its rocky hackles.

Spring intimates its presence. A duet of red-winged blackbirds in the frozen willow: a spackling of green shoots in the snow aureole of a sun-warmed boulder; a willow branch sprouts downy catkins beside the lilting freshet in the canyon by the clay banks.

Spring lures children to the meadowlark's trill, to Chapman's field to cast their motley kites before the wind. Messages spin, twist their way up the looping string, up, up into the kite's embrace. Chasing its tail, an aerial cat, the kite dips and darts, its playful tugs plaiting kite string and heartstring, the eternal bonding of youth and spring.

We scoured the hills looking for spring. Even before the snow left the shaded spots, we searched, sought spring on the southern slopes where the snow was first to melt. We found spring in the canyon, sprouting gray and furry from the greening willows. Spring made us charitable. We gathered the thickest, most turgid catkins from the willows, snipped the branches with their burgeoning litters of buds and presented these first spoils of spring to our mothers. We roamed the sage and greasewood flats, the rockpiles, ever vigilant for infant sprouts, dainty fronds unfurling from a crevice in a sunwarmed rock. Far afield we ventured, the winds of promise in our faces. We frolicked in the lengthening hours of daylight until the plaintive lilt of a double-barreled whistle drifted up from the river below, calling us home: Kevin, a solitary blast; Tim, two toots; Claudia, three; I headed home at four; five forlorn hoots sprung us all from the wilderness, home on the run.

Those days were jacket days; we shed them quickly enough once the west winds subsided and the day took the sun seriously. Spring returned us to our favorite haunts: Chief Joseph's Rock, a flat, lichen covered granite slab suitable for picnics on a tilt; Crevice Rock, a cleft boulder through which you could pass between the two halves, or duck between them if you wanted to hide from a seeker; and Pond Rock, so termed because of the numerous depressions gouged into its surface by some glacial, or perhaps, pre-glacial forces. These hollows filled with rainwater or snow melt, creating small ponds, thus its namesake. Pond Rock, on its south side, thrust itself above the range land like a miniature Ayers Rock. This landmark was a far jaunt from home, and you had to confront two barbed wire fences to reach it. The rock was on Whitley land, and we were always nervous playing there, expecting Kenny Whitley, on horseback, to ride up at any moment, and order us off his property. Whitley was very territorial and did not suffer trespassers, especially dogs, for which he set out poison bait, though he maintained the poison was for marauding coyotes, threats to his livestock. I don't know if the baits were effective to that end, but they were death on dogs. Kevin's black Lab Tor fell victim to the bait during one spring excursion to Pond Rock. I helped my little brother carry his dead pet home, its gangly body yet warm, mouth still frothing. The incident enraged and saddened our family. So much for trespassing.

The Spring Thaw

The winters we had snow packs, when the clear, sunny days of late February came, the snow would melt and deliver spring to the valley in a rush of flood water, mud, and debris. At night the temperatures would dip into the low twenties, freezing the ground in the gullies and canyons, a shallow permafrost impervious then to next day's snowmelt. Watercourses that barely trickled the rest of the year became roaring torrents of ruddy water. Where these met the county roads, they became studies in alluvial fans, depositing deltas of gravel and silt three and four feet thick across the highway, halting traffic and creating a frenzy among the county road crews.

Traffic meant the school bus, and until the county plows could clear the roads, we were without transportation to school. I was not one to let a spring thaw interfere with my education—or recess with my friends—and as foot traffic was the only option, hiked the four miles to school and back. I only remember skipping school one day in all my school years on the river. One hunting season I was lured afield by an abundant supply of upland game birds. The next day Mom wrote me an excuse claiming I had been "indisposed."

Though I didn't know the meaning of the word, the term satisfied school authorities and my "hooky" play went without consequence. (One time I left school early and walked home. I needed some leverage in a romantic misunderstanding and told my girlfriend Irene Dachel I was leaving school on account of our falling out. I had hoped to reduce her to tears with this pronouncement, which I did, but in retrospect, I realize her tears sprung from embarrassment, not from a broken heart: I had humiliated Irene in front of her friends.)

One February a flashflood swept wall to wall down the canyon and backed up against the county road where the forty-eight inch culvert was overwhelmed by the onslaught of water. A huge whirlpool formed ahead of the culvert, and among the flotsam whirling in the vortex was the trunk of a tree nearly the size of my leg. When I left my vantage point, that section of tree was still twisting in the muddy whirlpool as if someone was stirring a giant Bloody Mary. The flood compromised the road bed, and later county crews had to replace the smaller culvert with one large enough to allow passage to future spring torrents. Downstream the flood washed out the access road to Riverview Ranch. You could hear the roar of the flood from our front yard a quarter mile away.

The Wildflowers of Spring

Whan that Aprill with his shoures soote,
The droghte of March hath perced to the roote,
And bathed every veyne in swich licour
Of which vertu engendred is the flour...

Chaucer
Prologue to the Tales of Canterbury

In early spring we sought the first wildflowers among the sage and greasewood, the floral treasures of the hills, the manifestations of spring. On the south slanting hills we were greeted by the buttercups (*Ranunculus glaberrimus*), the first wildflowers of the new year. The golden glint of this short stemmed, five petaled flower freckling the greening pasture slopes warmed you as much as the spring sun. Even for small fists the stems were too short for gathering bouquets, so like young Midas's we would pluck one at a time, twirl the stems between our fingertips and delight in their golden sheen. We spun them until their stems collapsed, cast them away, and fetched up more.

We knew the haunts of our favorite flowers: when they could catch the full sun, buttercups in open spaces. Others seemed to prefer the company of a sagebrush and would sprout beneath its protective branches. The most dainty of these we called "babyfaces" (though guidebook taxonomy terms them "Prairie Stars" [*Lithophragma parviflorum*]), perhaps because their ruddy centers were like a newborn's bonneted face, surrounded by delicate, serrated petals. Each diminutive, chaste face perched on a long tender stalk, which sometimes threaded its way through the low hanging limbs of a protective sage. These we gathered until we had a fistful and then homeward to our mothers where we offered up our filigreed handfuls as if they were bundles of lace.

Sometimes we complemented our babyface bouquets with "shooting stars" (*Dodecatheon pulchellim*) or "birdbeaks," so termed because of the dark purple pointed bases extending from the swept back pink petals. These odd-shaped primroses commingled with the babyfaces. Though not always in the company of sage, they preferred damp, mossy seeps. Shooting stars were long-stemmed, easy to gather, and a fistful of these beauties always brought exclamations of pleasure from our mothers.

We could gather a medley of spring flora by adding bluebells (*Merensia ciliata*) to the mix. These plants blossomed with tubular, bell-shaped flowers, also grew in the company of shooting stars and babyfaces, and like the latter preferred to nestle beneath a sheltering sage. The bells grew in clusters, blending blue with lavender, at times pink-hued. Bluebells were harder to bouquet because of their short stems, which you had to nip off nearly below the surface in order to have enough stem to grasp. I can still feel the gentle buffeting the bells gave my fist as I jostled down hillsides one cow trail to the next.

The rarest of spring wildflowers–and my favorite–were the yellow bells (*Fritillaria pudica*). Gathering them was like seeking gold nuggets—or perhaps a more apt comparison—truffles. Members of the lily family, yellow bells presented one demure yellow bell-shaped flower per plant. Their blooms were short-lived; you could easily miss their bloom cycle if you did not search for them weekly in April. I don't believe a blossom lasted much beyond a week and recall being disappointed to find every bell-shaped flower in the patch a shrunken ruddy brown. Those years I came away with no bouquets. Not only did you need perfect timing to catch a plant in bloom, but you had to look in just the right sageland niche to find a yellow bell patch. All the years I spent combing the hills for this comely little flower, I found only three patches. They seemed to flourish on the rocky, cobbled brow of a south slanting hill, but you could not always find them there. Stumbling across a patch was serendipitous, and once you found one, you knew just where to look next spring, and then gathering them only required timing. Orchards now grow where two of the patches bloomed. The third, my secret patch, still blooms, I'm sure, each April down Dougherty Canyon.

The most yellow bells I ever saw at one time Carol Kimball had clasped in her hand. A schoolmate of mine, and one year my senior, Carol and I rode the same school bus. One spring she carried, in what must have been a very cramped hand by the time she arrived at school, a bouquet of fifty or so yellow bells, a gift of gold to her teacher. I asked Carol where she found such a prolific site, certainly the mother lode of all patches. She replied evasively, "Oh, in the hills." She had staked her claim and was not about to let it be jumped by a schoolmate. Years later after my wildflower forays were done, I kept bees on her mother's property and during routine maintenance on my colonies one spring, I stumbled on Carol's secret lily cache. But alas for us both, the patch is now orchard. Cherry trees, I believe.

There was no finer way to participate in spring than to comb the greening hills for wildflowers. And by gathering fistfuls of flowers and carrying them home, I could share spring with Mom, who because of domestic duties, was housebound and a shut-in.

Lag Up

...and eddieandbill come
running from marbles and
piracies and it's
spring...

e.e.cummings

On my way to work in the mornings I was in the habit of stopping at a convenience store to buy the daily paper. This was early in the morning, usually before 7:00 a.m. As I entered the door, immediately the synthesizer cacophony of electronic games assaulted my ears. Kids, that early in the morning, before school, would be cramming quarters into those machines like tossing crumbs to pigeons in the park. Then I would think of a simpler time when all a kid needed to exercise (aside from shoving quarters into a slot), and entertain himself for hours were a dusty school playfield, a classmate or two, recess, and a pocket full of marbles.

The first appearance of bare ground (mud, usually) showing through the snow brought the onset of marble season. I remember blowing warmth into my blushing fist, fingers aglow after retrieving my errant shooter from one snowmelt puddle after another. I remember the difficulty of taking aim through the distracting fat flakes of a March snowstorm. And I remember marbles swallowed up by a snowbank, lost forever.

Our marble season lasted from the first early spring contest until the end of school in May, a season much the duration of any major sport. And as other sports, marbles had its own rules and jargon (a glossary of which concludes this section).

In marbles, unlike other sports involving a sphere, the glassy orb had both aesthetic and sentimental value to a player. I thought some marbles too beautiful to chance losing in a game. (The game of marbles was an acquisitive sport; you played for keeps.) The first time I saw a cat's eye, I thought it worthy enough to be a crown jewel. When held to the light, clearies or puries presented a fiery orb at their centers. Some marbles appeared opaque, but when you held them to the sun, you were surprised by a translucence that betrayed the true color. I owned such a marble for years and would delight in the purple iridescence which blazed forth each time I passed it before the sun. Clearies were seldom clear, usually displaying a spray of tiny bubbles in their depths. Made from agate stone, aggies were murky, turbid—not a pretty marble—valued as a shooter because of their heft. These we rarely ever saw; I never owned an aggie myself until long after my playing days were done. The least desirable marble was fashioned from some ceramic or porcelain material, shaped and then kiln-fired, I believe. Their surfaces bubbled in the firing process, resulting in a honeycombed, pocked surface. Though some were an attractive blue, these crockery marbles were hardly ever traded, and usually the last to leave the marble ring. And there were the steelies, of course, which were just that—ball bearings masquerading as marbles.

Though we admired, coveted, and safeguarded the exotics, no marble had a greater sentimental value than your shooter. The shooter was your "gamer." The success of the season, your entire marble fortune, rested on it: therefore you chose your shooter carefully. Feel or heft was important. When your thumb was cocked, the shooter nestled against the fleshy porch of the knuckle and ball of the forefinger, felt like it belonged there, as Zen would have it, achieving oneness with those two digits. If you were careful to keep your shooter from harm's way, it served you well season after season. My shooter, a medium-sized marble, emerald-green, its surface scarred like a lunar landscape, had been around the block a few times. My thumb was acquainted with every chip, every scar on its surface. Though hardly an object of beauty, my shooter was as formidable an orb of glass as the best, and when we hunkered down to play, we were game for all comers.

Marbles ranged in size from BBs to boulders. Between these extremes, from small to large, came pee-wees and regulation size marbles—used both as shooters and daters. Next, a mid-size variety somewhere between the regulation marble and boulder.

My shooter was a mid-sizer. A player's basic outlay of glass capital came in bags from the store, though I believe some variety of breakfast cereal used a small bag of cat's eyes as a promotional gimmick. You increased your inventory by skill on the field of play. Trading usually reduced inventory: you coveted a certain marble, steelie, or boulder, and your stock decreased according to desire. A third way you could increase your stock (more of this later) required the carelessness of a classmate, the beneficence of Mrs. Moore, and her novel way of disposing of confiscated marbles.

I stockpiled my marbles in a large coffee can. Each morning before school I would routinely count out my marble quota for the day and pocket it along with my shooter. Other kids carried their marbles in an old sock knotted loosely to confine the contents. Others had marble pouches, homemade mostly from levis and khaki cloth; some fancier ones of leather, with drawstrings to knot the top. With pocket storage you ran a greater risk of spillage. Restless squirming in your seat during the arithmetic lesson sometimes caused your pants pocket to ride up, tumbling your day's winnings to the floor. My parsimony carried over to my marble stash: I never took more to school than I was prepared to lose in a day's gaming. If I had a streak of bad luck or came up against stiff opposition, (one of the bigger kids, a sixth-grader, maybe), and lost my day's quota, the rest was safe at home. Though this happened rarely, when it did, I became a bystander, a student of the game the remainder of the day. Home from school, I would compare the contents of my pocket with the morning's quota, tally my winnings or lament the losses, and return the remainder to the can. (I was a fairly competent player and managed to keep the coffee tin two-thirds full, full enough anyway for a mouse to venture into the can one night, shove a marble over the rim, and entertain itself by rolling its plaything about the room.)

At recess during the height of the marble season, we had a game going on every corner of the playground. Clusters of boys stood or hunkered around a ring scratched in the dirt, each in turn vying for the glass loot at its center. Though dodge ball was coed, marbles, like football, was a man's sport. The girls were off somewhere skipping rope, scooping up jacks, or clambering on the monkey bars. Who cared? Time enough for romance in the off season. Marbles was serious play, and once in season, there was no time for frivolous sport like daring Jerilyn Eversson to hang by her knees from the monkey bars in hopes she had another hole in her underpants.

Regardless which species of marbles we played, the same ritual preceded each contest: lagging up, game protocol to determine who took the first shot. Someone would scratch a line in the dirt, back off another eight or ten feet, and scratch a second. The first line was the lag line. Each player would toe up to the second line, and either roll or toss his shooter toward the lag line. The owner whose marble came to rest closest to the line took the first shot, the next, the second, and so on till the rotation was set. (Like the batting order in baseball, the shooting order was set for the entire game.) My only sports nickname derived from this ritual. Football had its "Refrigerator" Perry, basketball its "Meadowlark" Lemon, baseball its "Yankee Clipper," and marbles had me, "T-Lagger," which later corrupted into "T-Legger." This aka was given me by my friend Dennis Gragg who had a nickname for everything—and everyone— (even his mother whom he called Eva-Butt and got away with it because she was hard of hearing and poor at lip-reading). After lagging up, the game began in earnest.

The object of marbles, of course, was to use one's shooter to knock all the marbles out of the pot or the playing circle. Before the first shooter took his turn, each player had to date up. This step was equivalent to "anteing up" in that other popular game of chance— poker; instead of cash you tossed a date in the center of the ring. The more players, the sweeter the pot; the more marbles in the ring, the greater your chances of knocking a couple out. When we lacked players, sometimes we agreed to double date or double our ante. Daters were regular marbles, ones you could afford to lose. But as in life, one man's trash is another's treasure: at least one player always seemed to date up a marble we preferred to go after first. When the first shooter took his turn, the game began.

Once the game was in progress, we abided by an unwritten set of rules. You became the "shooter" when your turn came round, and you shot until you failed to knock a marble from the ring. The prey had to be knocked entirely clear of the circle. If your marble came to rest on the line, we cried "liners!"and your turn abruptly ended with you basically putting another marble in the next opponent's pocket, as it would take little more than a nudge to knock it from the line. "Fudgies" was strictly forbidden, and we watched each other's fists with a critical eye for infractions. Then "No Fudgies!" or "Fudger" echoed across the playground, to the effect you lost your turn, composure, and perhaps reputation. Your turn continued if you knocked a marble from the ring and your shooter "stuck" (remained in the circle), a fortunate situation caused by hitting a marble square on, or if your shooter had a backspin on it. When the players cleaned the pot, the game was over, the one caveat being the school bell signaling the end of recess. Then a player would yell, "Grab dates and run!" The game ended abruptly and the entire pot was up for grabs, the remaining marbles scooped up and pocketed by whoever grabbed them first. The confines of recess led to this scenario, and we learned to monitor our time carefully to keep these free-for-all endings infrequent.

Marbles offered us a great deal of variety, and I remember the following versions to be our favorites. Round pots was the most traditional form of the game. The diameter of the circle or pot provided variety in and of itself. The large ring we called "large pots" or "bullrings." The circumference from that point was arbitrary: a ring too large made for a slow game; too small, the first shooter could "clean the pot" with any luck at all while the rest of us stood by watching all our marbles disappear into his pocket. On average, a circle with a diameter of three feet we considered the acceptable format.

One game we called square pots, a term, when you think about it, seems an oxymoron. Square pots featured a one foot square scratched in the dirt. We dated up a marble on each corner of the square and proceeded to play. I cannot recall the object of this game; unlike round pots, it was not to knock a marble "out" since the dates were placed on the four corners, nearly out anyway. Perhaps we began the game a number of steps from the pot, the lag line, maybe, and then as in golf, proceeded shot by shot toward the pot as if it were a putting green until we were close enough to whack the dates from the corners. Though I recall playing the game frequently, neither my brothers, friends, nor I remember any of the particulars of square pots.

Another favorite of ours was "Poison," a variety of marbles that combined the concepts of croquet and golf. In this version the course was a four or five foot square. At each corner of the square we scooped a shallow hole in the playground dirt. We scooped a fifth hole at the center of the square. We dated up in this center hole. The first shooter shot from a predetermined line toward the closest hole on the right. The object of the game was to proceed counterclockwise cup by cup around the square. After you successfully sank your shooter in the fourth cup, you shot for the center hole. If you sank your shooter there, then you became "poison," and as in croquet, you went after everyone else's shooter. (If you were unfortunate enough to strike a "poison" marble, you were out of the game.) You kept your turn until you missed a cup, or if you were poison, an opponent's shooter. The poison player whose shooter was never touched by an opponent, the last player to strike the only remaining shooter, won the game. And since poison was a game for "all the marbles," the loot in the center hole was yours to pocket. Our poison courses required time and effort to construct, and for these reasons we kept them in place for most of the season. A game of poison could consume a large amount of recess time, so we usually reserved a game for lunch recess when we had nearly an hour to do battle, so to speak, in the trenches.

If you wanted a less intense game of migs, you could always play "chasies," a version of the game where your marble chased your partner's around the entire playground—or world, for that matter. To play chasies all you needed was a partner. I don't remember more than a pair of us at a time ever playing the game. You would pocket your shooter for safekeeping and use an expendable marble instead. The object of the game was to strike, tap, nudge, or somehow touch your opponent's marble, which you then pocketed. An aggressive player would go right after his partner's shooter. This strategy, though exciting, was risky play. On the other hand, you might take a defensive approach: when your turn came, you tried to put as much distance as you could between your shooter and his. If your partner played conservative chasies, you could bait him by plunking your marble near his, tempt him to take a potshot. This tactic could easily backfire if your shooter plopped down closer than you wished. Then your pocket would be one marble lighter.

The only hard and fast rule in chasies (fudgies was ignored unless your lie was two feet or closer to your opponent's because you might want to flip your shooter twenty feet or so away) concerned the lie of your shooter: like golf, you had to play it as it lay. This condition made for great variety in a game. We played chasies in gravel, sand, and dust of a road, across irrigation ditches, through the litter of orchard leaves and brush, in and out of puddles, but wherever your marble came to rest, there it stayed until your turn to shoot—your opponent's concern, not yours. A marble might disappear under a leaf, bury itself in the dust, or roll into a puddle. The only strategy left you then would be to bring your opponent out of hiding by flipping your shooter in the opposite direction when your turn came. We played chasies to cool down after a day of intense marble wars, our last chance of the day to pad our pockets with more winnings. Our marbles were out as soon as the bus slowed for our stop, ready to chase one another down the long driveway, perhaps to arrive safely home with him that brought you—or in the pocket of a stranger.

The technique and strategy used in the game made the difference between mediocre play and success. The anatomy of a shot determined both the shooter's accuracy and ballistics: in short, it mattered how you held your shooter. A player used one of two methods to shoot a mig. In one method the player levered his shot by cocking the thumbnail under the forefinger and squeezing the shooter between the second and third knuckle. In this configuration the knuckles of the fist were positioned perpendicular to the ground. His shooter set, thumb cocked, the shooter then flicked his marble toward the target. This method had its drawbacks: it produced an awkward shot; the marble's trajectory was in a straight line roll until it stopped; if the player had a weak thumb, he was likely to fudge his shot; and it marked you as a beginner—you shot like a sissy. This method was analogous to throwing a straight ball in bowling, likewise to mediocre effect. The good marble players shunned the thumbnail method.

If you wanted to excel at marbles, you perfected the second method, a technique that brought your shooter to life, allowed you to put a spin on your game. In this configuration you cocked your thumbnail under the second and third knuckle of the index finger and rested your shooter high up on the thumb knuckle, squeezing it between knuckle and the tip of the forefinger, the back of your hand parallel to the ground. If you followed the procedure correctly, you were able to roll the shooter between finger and thumb instead of simply squeezing it in the crook of the forefinger. Such a grip allowed you to put a spin on your shooter when it left your fingers. The more you rolled the marble to the side of your thumb, the greater spin you gave it coming off that digit. Back to the bowling analogy: this technique paralleled throwing a hook ball to create the English necessary to cause maximum havoc among a set of pins. Not only did this method improve your aim, but it allowed you to give your shooter a mind of its own. If a player had a strong thumb, he could create a backspin on his shooter, make it "stick" in the pot while knocking a marble from the ring. You would hear a sharp click, a marble (sometimes two or three if the pot was heavy with dates) would fly from the ring, and in its place was the kid's shooter, spinning like a top. Whenever this happened, a groan of despair issued from the players. Now the kid had another turn: the fox was in the henhouse, the whole pot up for grabs. I've seen a player "clean a pot" like a pool shark running the table his backspin was so effective. Neil Shenyer, a tall, rangy kid and classmate of mine, had sinews and tendons like steel in his fingers. I've seen Neil's shooter strike a marble with such force it split in two, sending both halves flying from the circle. Neil could put a spin on a marble, make it stick—even roll backwards toward him. A shooter really came to life in Neil's hand. A marble marvel he was indeed. Even kids two or three grades older fell victim to that incredible backspin, were reluctant to do battle with the "little" kid. No need to tell you what shooting technique Neil used.

To confound or fluster your marble partners and sway advantage your way, you could reach into your marble bag of tricks and pull out a defensive strategy or two. One of these we called "changies." That's where those valuable steelies you acquired through trade came into play. Through the ploy of changies, you could exchange a larger or smaller marble for your dater, or if you thought it prudent, your shooter. You brought this strategy into play especially when a competitor stuck his shooter in the pot and your dater was his next victim. Then to break his stride, you cried, "Changies!" This maneuver brought the game to a halt while you fetched your steelie from the depths of your pocket. (If it weren't for the changies maneuver, steelies would have been a bother. As it was, you had to cinch your belt an extra notch just to keep your pants up if you lugged one of these around all day.) The act of exchanging a golf ball-size ball bearing for a glass marble effectually saved your bacon. No experienced player would pit his shooter against a steelie's mass. Though a direct hit might budge the ball bearing a smidgeon, your shooter would either chip or split in half. If it did survive the collision, most certainly the shooter ricocheted from the ring in a twinkling, as if it were something odious spat out by the steelie, a speedy reversal of fortune for the player who now not only came away empty but lost his turn and perhaps his shooter to boot. The experienced player knew he had to direct his next shot at another target, leaving your marble safe for the moment. (I believe you had to "change back" the proxy marble before you took your next turn.)

If he saw he had a good lie and his turn continued, a player nimble of mind could preclude the changies scenario by quickly blurting, "No Changies!"

Another changies move might be to substitute the size and mass of a steelie for a much smaller target, say a BB. Here you hoped your opponent would not be able to hit and knock the smaller object from the pot. This strategy was well-suited for cha-sies. In certain situations, you might want to use changies to switch your shooter for a larger marble, pit one boulder or steelie against another. If you thought a twig or some other hazard interfered with your shot, you were quick to invoke the "overs" rule. Again, a quick thinking opponent could counter with a "No Overs" of his own. If the marble ring presented obstacles that might deflect your shot— a pebble, depression, or bump—you would elevate your shot by resting your shooting hand on the back of your other, tilt it up on fingertip, and shoot over the obstruction. The chief end of all these strategies, of course, was to cut your marble losses.

Since we played for keeps, a player always risked losing some or all of his marbles. But a player needn't be involved in a game to lose his migs. While the game was a diversion on the playground, marbles in the classroom were anathema to our teachers. If you were caught counting your winnings during the lesson, you lost your marbles. If your marbles escaped because your sock had a hole in the toe (this occurred frequently to the sock bearers, as a good pair of socks belonged on the feet) you lost your marbles. If they somehow leaked from your pocket, they were goners. The rapid fire rat-tat-tat of a handful clattering about on the hardwood floor caused a cataclysm in the classroom. "Incoming!" and the Mrs.'s Moore, Davis, or Greaves would leap into action, snatch the offend-ing ordnance from our hands and stockpile it in a desk drawer.

Our first-grade teacher Mrs. Moore, the patron saint of us marble players, must herself have played migs in another life and gave us the opportunity to regain our lost loot. In two or three weeks' time our marble infractions yielded up nearly enough mar-bles to fill a mason jar. (Our other teachers may have contributed their "winnings" to the pot.) One day Mrs. Moore would inform her class a marble drop was imminent during noon recess. No other pronouncement could have spread as quickly through the school. No matter if the lunch entree was barbecued hamburger on buns, we would postpone or forego lunch to man our positions in the drop zone. Waiting impatiently for Mrs. Moore to finish her leisurely lunch, not for a second taking our eyes off the second story windows of her classroom (which one would she open this time?), we milled about below. Suddenly a window would slide up and a smiling Mrs. Moore would lean out, holding the treasure jar like a trophy. We would break ranks and jockey for a new position. Then the cascade of colored hailstones, and we were upon them. In a flurry of dust and elbows and fists we scooped up the marbles, every last one. Our possessions (and those of our schoolmates) reclaimed, we dusted ourselves off and beat it to the lunchroom. The next two weeks the marbles would shift possession again—from our pockets to Mrs. Moore's jar—until they were offered up once more from her classroom window. And so went the marble season.

A MARBLE GLOSSARY

aggie—a marble made from agate stone, heavier than a glass marble, therefore valued as a shooter

BB—a tiny marble or small ball bearing, usually the gauge of an air rifle pellet, used in game strategy; esp. changies

boulder—a golf ball-sized marble, either glass or metal

bullrings—a marble game using a two to three foot circle or ring as the pot; the place where such a game is played

cat's eye—a clear marble with a twist of color at its center, resembling the iris of a cat's eye

chasies—a marble game played by two players, the object being to hit the opponent's shooter by chasing it hither and yon

clean the pot—term used when a single player knocks out all the marbles in the pot in a single turn

clearie–a translucent, mono-colored marble; a purie

date/dater–a marble a player dates up in order to participate in the game; the player's share of risk in a game of marbles; his ante

date up–the act of placing a marble or marbles in the pot so a player can participate in the game at hand

fudgies–a breach of marble protocol whereby a player's shooting hand enters the plane of play before the shooter is released

fudger–a player who fudges his shot; with repeat offenders, synonymous with "cheater"

grab dates and run–a cry given by a player at the bell ending recess, allowing him to snatch up all remaining marbles in the pot before the end of the game; a practice possibly inspired by the fear of being tardy to class

lag line–in a game of marbles an arbitrary line to determine the order in which players take their turns

lag up–in a game of marbles a procedure used to determine the sequence of turns; the first step in a game of marbles

liners–the situation created in a game of marbles when a shooter or dater comes to rest on the line determining the field of play; a cry to indicate such a lie

marbellies–a slang term for marble, a game of marbles; migs

migs–a slang term for marbles or a game of marbles; origin unknown

overs—a cry permitting a player to repeat his shot, usually invoked because of interference

pee-wee—a marble a size halfway between a BB and a dater, used in game strategy; esp. changies

poison—a marble game in which the field of play is a rectangle having a hole or cup at each corner and a center hole used as the pot

pot—in the game of marbles the term for an arbitrary circle enclosing the field of play; the contents of such of a circle

purie—a translucent, mono-colored marble; a clearie

round pots—a game of marbles in which the field of play is a circle or ring

shooter—the special marble a player uses to strike or knock dates from the circle of play; one who uses a shooter; a player whose turn it is to shoot

square pots—a marble game in which the field of play is a square instead of a circle

steelie—a steel marble, usually a ball bearing, obtained by a player lucky enough to know a mechanic or machinist; used in game strategy; esp. changies

stick/sticking—in marbles a situation in which a player's shooter knocks a marble from ring, yet remains in the playing circle, allowing the shooter to continue his turn

FISH AND FLIES

May came. No month, excepting December with its glory days, held more promise. May brought great changes and signaled more. The river began to swell with the spring snow melt, the water glacial, the color of cold. The island is but a memory, drowned now, marked by a boiling current rushing over its head. Afternoon air, delicious with warmth, fraught with lilac, ponderous with fragrance, pressed heavy on the riverbank. May crowned the apple trees a blushing white, their blossoms plundered by frenzied bees. Those long, languid days, the end of school and the summer solstice knocking on the door, we dawdled over our lessons, daydreamed river thoughts, reveries of water and current, the miracle of the river. Those May afternoons the school bus seemed oblivious to the river's siren call, ignored our impatience, and took its own sweet time carrying us to the bus stop where we would tumble over each other exiting the door. Down the driveway pell-mell to a vantage point above the river, we began the afternoon vigil. As the river curled by, we studied the banks, every wrinkling eddy, every sportive whirl. We scouted the water, on guard for the tell-tale movement above the current. But the river withheld, and we scuffed our way home disappointed. Afternoons, one upon the other, this was our ritual those early days in May. And then one warm day, as the afternoon breeze gently lifted the down from the cottonwoods and set it adrift upon the wind, the miracle arrived.

The flight began mid-afternoon, around three o'clock. Soon the river air was a swarm of insects, thousands, tens of thousands of them. The air turned palpable, heavy with the flutter of a million soft wings. The salmon fly hatch was on.

Barely an inch long, the adult salmon fly by itself was at best nondescript. Unlike the seductive beauty of most lepidoptera, the bug's metamorphosis from egg to adult ranged aesthetically from ugly to plain. Its body enclosed by two dun-gray wings, set on dihedral, the fly was drab, moth-like. But when the bug took flight along with a myriad of its kin, the result was awesome. Their flyway formed a corridor three to four feet high above the river, and this space teemed with flying bodies. Launching themselves from rocks and willows, they began an upstream flight, beating their way inexorably upriver against the breeze. You sensed method in their flight, a sense of urgency, a solidarity of purpose: they knew their destination, struck out for it; and all strove to arrive at once. If you stood on the bank, an obstacle among them, they pelted your face, a pummeling of soft bodies. Some would collide with your clothing, and addled, cling a moment, then hurl themselves into flight again.

We knew little of the natural history of these insects. It was their effect, which I'll relate in a moment, that caused such a stir among us. No doubt they were some sort of ephemerid, some species of caddis, perhaps, a smaller cousin of the Mayfly, but having little in common with them than the month of May. We knew them by no other name than *salmon fly*, and the role the insect played in the river's ecology, if it concerned the river's salmon population, I don't know. I am no wiser about the term's origin today.

In general, we knew each insect spent the rest of the year submerged, its larval form incubating in a sand-encrusted tube glued to a river cobble. We also knew each adult female exuded a bluish-green egg sac, gooey, pill-like, from its abdomen. But just how an egg in that sac ended up a worm encapsulated in a sand tube was a mystery to us. Just as mysterious was the ecological stimulus that triggered the hatch. Was it the rise in water level? Snow-melt induced–the lowering of water temperatures? Or was it simply chronological: their time to be born into the air? We did not know then, nor do I now. What I do know is once the Well's Dam hydroelectric project was completed, the riverbank disappeared in lake, and with the change so did the mid-May phenomenon of the salmon fly exodus and its associate miracle. A new ecology replaced the old, and now the bugs of May take flight no more.

As determined as they were, great numbers of salmon flies never reached their destination, nor did they complete their reproductive cycle. The naturalist Darwin, I believe, observed that for a species to perpetuate itself, it must produce a prodigious amount of offspring to counter the predators certain to nip quantities of young–or adults–in the bud before they reproduced. This theory proved itself every May by pitting the fecund power of the salmon fly's egg sac against the Columbia River whitefish. The miracle of May was one of cause and effect. It was quite simple: the whitefish came for the salmon flies, and we came for the whitefish.

Every jut of bank created an eddy, and in every eddy frolicked a school of feeding whitefish. The current swung out from the bank, carrying with it a flotilla of downed salmon flies, thereby creating a continuous soup line for the whitefish, who swallowed them by the mouthful with minimum effort. No sooner had the afternoon's hatch begun, than each eddy became a cauldron of frenzied fish, a tail slapping, somersaulting pool of silver glory. You could see the commotion a good distance up the bank. Then the cry, "The whitefish are jumping!" And we would gather up our fishing gear, rush to the river and join the show.

While the hatch was on, neither skill nor guile was required to catch a whitefish. No need to experiment with lures or bait. Or resort to stealth. Nor did you have to play the waiting game. The fish came to you, a whole river full right before your eyes, just spoiling to be yanked from the water. It was "in your face" fishing. Talk about instant gratification–everyone a fisherman! All you needed for gear was a hook, six or seven feet of line, and a stick or pole to attach it to. (One season I used a six foot cottonwood sapling, cut a notch in the tip, and knotted a three yard length of monofilament to it.) In this scenario no need to ask, "What are they bitin' on?" You snatched a handful of bugs from the air, (maybe snagged one or two out of your ears or nose) scooped up a fistful of floaters, mashed them into a ball, which you sculpted around your hook. Then you deftly caught the edge of current with your cast and instantly "Kerwhack," you had a fish. You backed up the bank, landed it, whacked it once or twice in the head with a rock or a chunk of driftwood, removed the hook, and returned to the fray. Now if you were lucky enough to own an artificial fly—and there were those among us who did (though Puddy One-Eye cancelled me out in this arena)—you didn't have to waste time baiting your hook. A kid could do some serious fishing then.

The whitefish we pulled from the river were eight to four-teen inches long, their flesh firm, hardened by the frigid water. They were named, I'm sure, for their immaculate white bellies, but also for their rather large scales which flashed silver when they rolled and twisted in the backwaters of the eddy. High shouldered like an Arctic grayling (a similar species, I believe), but minus the mantilla-like dorsal fin, a bug fed whitefish was a scrapper. A large one would sometimes snap your line. An electric jolt thrilled up your arm and through your body when a fish took the hook and ran with it. In an evening of sport it was not unusual to land a dozen or more fish apiece. Then fashioning a stringer from a willow withe, we threaded the branch through the gills and out the mouth and packed home our catch where we faced the messy task of the evening—gutting the catch. (On the river we learned early the sportsman's creed: "You catch it, you clean it.") And to this day I can hear Aunt Avis's startled scream when a victim, not quite deceased, slapped the floor with its tail as I severed its head from the backbone.

It took just two nights on the bank for us to become fish poor: you can put away only so much fresh game. Besides, unlike steelhead, whitefish were bony eating; we soon tired of sifting each mouthful with tooth and tongue. A couple of courses of whitefish sated the piscatorial appetite. Some whitefish we froze. Others we unloaded on our friends and relatives. Soon the entire camp was saturated. When there were no more takers, our evening forays to the river shifted to the catch and release mode–true sportsmen knew better than waste game.

One curious note about our evening sessions with the whitefish: each night at twilight, the fish stopped jumping. The activity didn't just trail off either–it ceased instantly. One minute tail and fin would be cavorting among the drifting flies, the next gone, all of them, one final flip of fin and flop of tail. Where moments before there was a waiting line for your hook, now your line drifted slack. Cast after cast came up empty. It was like someone had thrown a switch, rang some underwater curfew bell. The suddenness of it nearly left us breathless.

Just as quickly as it began, the miracle ended. The storm clouds of insects disappeared. The whitefish survivors moved on. We stowed our fishing gear. Soon too, we would stow our school books. May was at an end. In its stead we had summer.

SUMMER

Summer time when the livin' is easy

Porgy and Bess

Swollen beyond its banks and big-bellied, the river presses heavy on the island. Dawn sidesteps the thunderclouds stacked against the east, eases by them, and spills into the valley, a gilded rose. A dove calls mournful, its complaint gentle on the morning air. From a distant telephone pole a flicker in counterpoint drums a hearty tattoo. And with one last yawn, the riverbank shrugs off sleep, and stretches to meet the summer day.

At evening, nighthawks, as if on roller coasters, climb through the bleeding sky, hang a moment upon it, then hurtle earthward, wrest a sonic boom from the startled air, and soar aloft again. Daylight falters, the river shot with quicksilver. In the easy backwater along shore a lone mariner strives against the current. The muskrat paddles

resolute, shouldering a lazy V across the pearled surface.
Wavelets dapple silver, lap against the current, smooth
and disappear. And through the soft twilight seeps the
Evening Star.

The school bus brought us home to summer. The thought of long, endless days ahead, untold adventures, and family vacations made us giddy. One year on the last day of school, our ecstasies drove us to delinquency: we became squirt gun terrorists and welcomed in summer by giving our bus mates a thorough soaking, a baptismal of the season. The two or three days before the crime were sweet with conspiracy. Three or four of my pistol packing friends and I comprised this terrorist crew; I believe I was the ringleader. During recess and on the bus to and from school, we ironed out the details and hatched a plan sure to produce the maximum effect with a minimum of consequence. Therefore, we decided to perpetrate our crime on the last day of school, on the final bus ride of the school year.

That morning we four "perps" climbed aboard the bus, each of us packing. Any nervousness or ill at ease would not betray us because our driver Bill Shenyer would be certain to dismiss such behavior as end of the year excitement. Part of our plan. We toted our weapons to school unloaded, the reason being, as every water pistol gunslinger knew, was the tendency of these plastic weapons to leak, causing a dark stain to spread from one's pocket dangerously close to the crotch. This stain could tip off the teacher, and before you knew it, you were quickly disarmed, and your weapon soon in the company of a handful of marbles in the teacher's desk. To one of your classmates, the stain in your groin area meant only one thing: the urge to share that fact with every other kid in class or on the playground. Unless we intended to use our weapons in the near future, we found it wise not to conceal a loaded weapon, keep our powder and our crotches dry.

The day school dismissed for the summer we rushed to the boys' lavatory, quickly filled our pistols at the sink, and rushed to catch the bus. We knew better than to rush our attack. Bill would stop the bus and make us walk home to summer. No, we planned to wait for the moment the bus slowed for our stop. Then we would leap into action. After we drained our weapons, we would stymie Bill's move to disarm us by throwing the pistols out the window into the ditch where we would reclaim them later. After all, we would need our arsenal for summer's recreation. As it was the last day of school, Bill could do little to punish us short of delivering a good chewing out; he could hardly forbid us from riding the bus the next day, could he? Three months down the road—well, even Bill would have forgotten the incident.

Just as the bus slowed, we sprang into action, drew our weapons, and opened fire, our fingers madly pumping away on the triggers. Our shooting was random; regardless of where a kid sat—in front or the rear—he was a target, a soaked victim. The streams of water brought squeals of distress from the girls and angry cries from the boys and pandemonium as everyone sought shelter. The brakes shrieked and simultaneously we flung our dripping guns from windows. We executed our daring plan without a hitch and as Bill strove to regain control of the drenched passengers, we exited the bus before he could nab us and fled down the driveway straight into summer.

This story has a post script. When the bus arrived that fall to carry us back to school, I discovered our derring-do had weighed heavily on Bill's mind over the summer. That first day of school he set me to walk the straight and narrow; he would tolerate no malfeasance on his bus this year and wanted to share this information with Dad next morning before I could ride the bus again. I would not be allowed on the bus until Bill and Dad had this parley. I never told Dad about the incident, was more afraid to face his displeasure than Bill's, and when Bill and the bus showed up the next morning, I told him that Dad couldn't take the time to escort me to the bus stop: he was too busy with harvest. Bill, himself a farmer, accepted the explanation and let me board the bus. Besides, I think he felt I was chastised enough, and he was not one to leave a kid standing at the bus stop in a cloud of dust and exhaust. I'm sure I engaged in other minor pranks over the years, but I have to state for the record that it was not I, but some other kid who shared the chocolate laxative with his fellow passengers. (The sudden charity made me leery—seemed odd a kid would just give away candy.) The next day the bus was nearly empty, and I thought it a waste of time and diesel for Bill to drive the route that day.

The Owl Thicket

In fact those summers on the river it seemed we were always armed with some weapon or other. We packed a jackknife, a bow and arrows, perhaps an air rifle, or sometimes only a pocket of rocks. Seldom, however, do I remember entering a summer without a slingshot.

You began your slingshot project in early spring, before the willows were in leaf. (Not having to contend with foliage made your search easier.) In late spring, floodwaters would cover the banks, and thickets would be inaccessible until midsummer. Your first challenge was to find just the right forked willow. The fork or crotch you sought needed to form a perfect V; both legs or prongs of the fork had to branch away from the crotch at the same angle. The V of the crotch had to be a suitable width: too narrow and you were likely to ricochet a rock off one of the legs; too far apart and you might bounce one off the handle. What you really wanted was a forked branch, each leg six or seven inches long, with a four to five inch spread from tip to tip across the top of the V. To find such a prize could take hours; perfection, we knew, was worth the wait— and summer deserved the perfect slingshot.

Once you had made several turns around the branch, scrutinized it from every angle, were confident you had found the best crotch in the thicket, you hacked the fork from the branch, leaving just enough stalk for a handle. You carried your prize home where you stripped the fork free of bark down to the gleaming wood. Then you rounded and smoothed the tips of the fork and handle and set the project aside to cure until summer.

The willow thicket most likely to yield that perfect forked branch was just upriver from the pump that brought irrigation water to the homeplace orchard. Because owls haunted it, we called this grove the Owl Thicket. One day in midsummer while I was threading my way through the dense center of the thicket, I discovered the owls. They were mewed up in the grove's secret center, two pair, off duty from their nocturnal patrols of the riverbank. The four were Great Horned owls, impressive in size, foreboding in appearance. From beneath the great tufted ears glared eight golden eyes. Startled, I stood in the gloom and returned their stares, outnumbered by eyes eight to two. It was as if I had stumbled upon a clandestine meeting of spirits, or like Macbeth, happened upon a coven of witches. They acted not in the least threatened by my presence, this creature who came crashing in on them. We tolerated each other across a space of eight or ten feet.

I soon saw they were as interested in me as I was them, and while they sat curious on their perches, I turned birdwatcher. It is said of owls that they can swivel their heads in a full circle. They can't, of course, but I watched them swivel their heads in remarkable ways. One moment an owl and I made eye contact, the next I was looking at the back of its head. Once I swear I saw one swivel its head a full three-quarter turn until its beak came to rest over its left shoulder. Soon I was laughing at the antics of these fierce-looking birds. When one swiveled its head and inverted eyes and beak, I really chuckled. I discovered each bird required a comfort zone of about six feet. When I invaded this space, it would fly—never far—just enough to reclaim a safe distance. The owls lived in the thicket from one summer to the next and falls too until the foliage left the branches, leaving the birds without cover. On those rare occasions when the action was slow on the riverbank, I would visit Owl Thicket and its tenants—those feathered clowns were always good for a laugh.

We were always on the lookout for castoff inner tubes; they provided an essential component of slingshot construction: the rubber that put the snap or "sling" in the slingshot. The mechanic's shop at the ranch had a supply of these, derelicts from tractors, trucks, and other ranch equipment. We scoured scrap heaps of broken machinery, discarded hoses, and other junk, looking for rejects. Those we located we brought to the camp mechanic, asked him which ones were beyond repair, could we have a couple and lugged home our keepers. Then a sharp pair of scissors, and we had our rubber catapult strips.

First, we would check the strips for elasticity. Many tubes had "dead" rubber, no snap or give to it whatsoever, completely useless for slinging stones—a waste of time fussing with these. The premium rubber came from red inner tubes. This was fast rubber and made for a lively slingshot. Red tubes were scarce, a rarity to find. If you did find one, you were quick to closet it away for safekeeping, several seasons' worth of slingshot material, your rubber reserves. Unless you could somehow talk a kid out of a couple lengths of his premium rubber, you had to settle for the black, the common grade stuff with inferior snap.

The most challenging step in slingshot construction was fastening the two rubber strips to the fork. First, you selected two pieces an inch or so wide—you didn't want them to snap in two—each long enough to accommodate your arm span: too long and you couldn't achieve maximum snap; too short, and your rock barely cleared the crotch. To prevent the rubber from slipping off the tip of the fork, you notched both tips with a shallow groove. The most difficult task came last: tying each length to the slingshot. You could not perform this step by yourself but had to enlist a second pair of hands. Either you or your helpmate looped the rubber around the notched tip. Careful not to use too much rubber, sure to keep both strips of equal length, you pressed both sides of the loop together, pinched hard and tugged. The other two hands took a length of string, quickly lashed two or three turns between your fingers and the wood, and tied it off before your grip gave out. The two of you repeated the procedure three more times: once on the second tip, twice more on the opposite ends to bind the strips to the patch of leather or denim used to cradle the stone projectile. It was imperative all four points be firmly lashed and tied. If the lashing failed while you were pulling to maximum draw, the entire sling apparatus would snap loose and fly back in your face with enough force to bring tears of pain and frustration. In the world of slingshots, such equipment failure was commonplace. My sister achieved a similar effect by executing the procedure backwards, stretching the carrier out in front of her, and then releasing it full force in her face. The physics of the thing weren't quite clear to her. But then it's hard to see through teary eyes.

With a little experience and patience, you ended up with a decent slingshot, not just a functioning weapon but a work of art. You took the thing, shoved it in your back pocket where it dangled jauntily the rest of the day. Then as you went about the day's business, you were just a stoop and a stone away from combat, be it with an unsuspecting tin can or bottle in the dump or some unfortunate songbird.

I don't believe our slingshots posed much of a threat to the local wildlife, though we did wreak considerable havoc with the mud nests the bank swallows constructed under the eaves of the cold storage shed. Our weapons were not very accurate, in part because the stones we chose were never round or smooth, making at best for errant ballistics. Some kids used their slingshots to dispose of their spring marble winnings, behavior I considered rash and profligate. Besides, their using marbles instead of rocks didn't seem to improve their marksmanship. I only killed one bird with a stone, an unsuspecting robin I pegged on the first throw—by hand, not with a slingshot. One minute Mr. Redbreast was making merry among the ripe fruit in a pie cherry tree, the next recumbent in the weeds beneath the tree, just a memory and a puff of feathers drifting in the air. I don't know which of us was more surprised.

Chores

Because summers offered the potential for unlimited play, thus the chance my siblings and I might revert to the wild, become feral children, Mom and Dad insisted we set aside an hour or two a day for chores. Through suffering we would learn to appreciate fully the gift of summer. Until we retired our daily duties, the day's play was held hostage. The object of the chores was for us to contribute to the operation of the household, teach us family citizenship; children, however, have a natural aversion to chores, and we were no exceptions. Perhaps it was the ominous sound of the word—**chores**—like a punitive sentence imposed because we were children. Unlike work, which implied some sort of reward: a salary or payment, chores were performed gratis—forced labor, and the only pleasure we derived from them was when they were behind us. Summers, we believed, were a child's birthright, an unequivocal reward for surviving the grueling routine of the school year. We viewed chores as an oppressive mandate, tantamount to revenge because adults themselves had to work.

Most chores were no different than those of our friends: routine swabbing out of our bedrooms and bathrooms, washing windows, sweeping the porches, taking out the trash, cleaning up after meals. And like most kids, we grumbled our way through these. As I was the oldest and biggest in the chain gang, one chore that was my lot in summer was yard maintenance. Mowing our lawns was an ordeal on several fronts. Every lawn on the ranch, Cranes' vast lawn included, was virgin to the power mower. Swathe by swathe I cut the grass pushing before me a reel type push mower; you pushed at the grass and the entire yard pushed back. Not only were the lawns bumpy and uneven, there was not one that didn't slope. You pushed downhill on the run and labored on the return trip, both grass and gravity against you. The long, narrow lower lawn had to be cut lengthways along the side slope, each pass a struggle to keep the mower on a straight line, fighting against the tendency to slip-slide downhill. The grass grew thick on this lawn, was clover-sotted. You leaned your whole body into the handles, sometimes having to retreat and run again at an unyielding patch. I remember many times my skinny arms stretched to their limit, my legs extended to tiptoe, stalled in the moment like a bizarre lawn ornament: the grass would not yield. Now my uncle Les liked novelty (he had a pet skunk named Stinky), had a piece of power equipment for every outdoor task around his lawn and small orchard, among them a gas-powered reel mower that nearly jerked your arms from their sockets when you engaged the clutch and then proceeded to drag you all over the yard. The power mower was a luxury surpassed only by Uncle Les's smooth, level lawn.

Often the aroma of the fresh clippings would trigger my asthma, and soon I'd be gasping for breath, leaning on the mower handles, not for leverage, but support. The lawn would have to wait until another day. One evening Dad came home from work and found me hanging from the mower handles, struggling for air. I must have been a pitiful sight because he told me to let the lawn be for the day, that if he could somehow transfer my affliction to himself, he would do it in a minute. I went wheezing into the house, grateful for my reprieve, comforted even more by the sentiment.

During soft fruit season, summer play was put on the back burner and the big enamel canner moved to the front, bubbling for action. Ours was a large family and the laying by of stores helped trim a dollar or two from the grocery bill. The big chest freezer on the back porch already boasted spring asparagus and pie cherries, all provender the ranch supplied for the gathering. Now we would add jars of canned fruit to the winter stores.

We used a routine division of labor, assembly line style, to prepare the fruit for the jars. First, one of us washed the fruit then passed it to the next station to be pitted. Pitting the fruit was my job. Wielding a sharp kitchen knife, I would slice through the buttocks seam of an apricot or peach, peel back the halves, extract the pit, and pass both sections along to the next station. Preparing the cots was easy work. Not so with peaches or pears. Peaches you immersed in boiling water for a few minutes so the skins would release from the flesh. After the scalded fruit cooled to the touch, you took each between your palms, twisted, and the skins would slough off. If the peaches were not quite ripe, the skins wouldn't slip, and you would have to pare the fruit, a time consuming frustration when you had better things to do, say swimming. Pears, which had to be peeled and then cored, were the most labor intensive fruit to prepare.

The cored and peeled fruit passed down the line to be layered and packed in Mason jars. This step required a specialist, Claudia, whose small hands fit easily through the mouth of the jar. She would place the halves of peach or pear or cot flat side down, layering one upon the other, packing each jar full to the neck. Then on to Mom who filled the jar with steaming syrup, applied the scalded rings and screwed them tightly to the threads. The jars, seven at a time, were arranged in a wire basket and lowered gently into the bubbling kettle. Thirty minutes later, as gently as before, they were lifted from the kettle to cool. The success of the entire operation came down to a metallic "plunk" and a dimpled seal, sure signs a jar had safely sealed.

Those hot August days and the steam from our canning made our small kitchen miserable, a steaming sauna; we nearly mopped the flesh from our foreheads. But no matter how uncomfortable, how exhausted our little assembly line became, each cheery ping, the sweet sound of success tempered our work, an audible affirmation our efforts, however tedious, had paid off. And though the tangible rewards would not come until winter meals, with each dimpled seal came a sense of satisfaction, a job well done.

The summer's most detestable chore also concerned summer produce: tending the family garden. (Given the hatred we had for this chore, I find it odd my siblings and I have a passion for gardening today. Perhaps this is so because we can garden on our own terms; then it was someone else's idea.) No other mandate made us cringe as much as Mom and Dad's saying, "I want you to work in the garden for an hour today." Or, "This afternoon, I want you to weed two rows of…"–the crop of the day about to be choked by weeds.

The family garden was a hot, dusty mile from home behind the planting we called the "80." This meant after the designated hour of stooping over rows of corn or beans, our backs seared by a relentless sun, we would have to plod the long distance home. After lunch we would meet the orchard crew at the shop and take the crew truck to the 80 where the workers would be thinning or propping. Even though beforehand we would tell the driver to stop at the garden, he would invariably forget, probably engaged in conversation with whoever was riding shotgun. But then we were kids, and no one paid much attention to us. The truck would fly by the garden carrying us to another stop further down the road. Then we would have to retrace the route on foot, already hot and tired, not a single weed yet pulled.

Once when the truck again rumbled on past the garden, I thought, "Enough of this," and jumped off. I hit the ground and immediately performed several impromptu cartwheels and somersaults like some dervish in a desert sandstorm. My gymnastics ended in the weeds alongside the road. The truck rolled on oblivious to my fate. At the time we were too timid to yell "Stop!" but after a few treks back through the dust and heat, we became surprisingly bold. When it was obvious we would fly by our stop, we would scream out in unison "Yo!" The driver would hit the brakes, tumbling all passengers against the headboard. But it was better to chance a bruise or two than to retrace that dusty road in the heat of the day.

I longed to expedite my garden chores by attacking the weeds with a hoe, but Dad thought I could not be trusted to wield the tool with precision, might slice away the sprouts of corn with an indiscriminate swipe of the blade. For me, it was pluck and pull the length of the row—real manual labor. After we had served our hour's sentence, stripped a couple of rows weed free, we began the tedious journey home, mocked by the afternoon sun. As I started the return trip, I would always say a silent prayer for Dad to come along, whisk me home in the jeep, cool my sweaty body in the breeze. But my prayers were seldom answered. After all, I was just a kid.

Swimming Lessons

Through the murky water of the lake the light seemed so far above me. My feet bounced off the bottom, but only my outstretched arm broke the surface. I sank. The light receded. I breathed in water. Once more I bobbed toward the light, tried to grasp it and pull my head into the air and breathe. Down again, inhaling only lake water. I was panicky now, trying to flail my way to the surface. The air was somewhere up in the light, hovering just out of reach. Just as I started under once more, someone grabbed me, pulled my head from the lake. Air and water contended in my throat and lungs. I coughed and spluttered to shore under Mom's arm, clasped firmly against her side like a dripping pup.

That's all I remember—or care to—of our summer vacation to Northern California. After hours of traveling in the shadow of Mt. Shasta, we decided to stop at Shasta Lake for a swim. I was nine years old, a non-swimmer, at the mud-crawling stage of water locomotion. However, that day I left the shallows and waded out up to my neck in the muddy water. And because I took one extra step, slipped into that drop-off, I was destined for swim lessons.

The Brewster and Pateros School Districts sponsored a summer swim program at Alta Lake. Kids living beside a body of water at times literally at their front door needed to learn to swim. Mom registered us all. I responded to swimming lessons as I did chore—I hated them. My Shasta Lake experience was imprinted vividly on my sinus cavities, and I feared water in my face and over my head.

On lesson days Mom would take us to the grade school where we boarded the bus to Alta Lake. Actually the lake was a pleasant reprieve from the summer heat—if only you didn't have to submerse your face in it. The temperature those dry afternoons hovered in the triple digit range; your hand flinched from the yellow paint below the open windows of the bus. Around the curves, through the stands of Ponderosa pine, the bus wound its way up out of the valley. In the swelter of the dry heat the spicy fragrance of sun-baked pine needles nearly overpowered us. As soon as the bus crested the hill and wound across the flat, I would crane my neck for the first glimpse of blue cupped between the rocky slopes and pine-sprinkled beach. Across the distance of three miles I could tell if I would dread the day's lesson or merely tolerate it. My hour of instruction would pass with little duress if the lake presented a tranquil aquamarine. If the lake shimmered, its surface a dance of diamonds, I shuddered. A wind was sweeping down lake, and I would spend an hour dodging wave slap, sure to make the return trip with lake water pooling stagnant in my sinus cavities. At Alta Lake the wind was always blowing.

The swim instructors were high school girls hired by the two districts. Paid to transform us from potential drowning victims into adept little paddlers, they subjected us to a variety of aquatic tortures. These included a bubble blowing routine that forced us to submerge our faces and exhale, the flutter kick, where to shouts of encouragement we churned the lake to a froth with our legs and feet, and the steamboat maneuver, which incorporated both techniques. In today's label-sensitive environment our group probably would have been given quaint animal names like "tadpoles," perhaps, but that summer we were lowly beginners, destined to grab handfuls of sandy bank and flutter kick away like fools. At least when you faced shoreward, you couldn't see the intermediate and advanced classes laughing.

As the summer progressed, our teachers would have us steamboat to a small raft a few feet from shore. Resting one hand upon the other, both arms outstretched as if in supplication, we would take a deep breath and kick away for the raft. This routine terrified me because to kick my way to the float, I had to steamboat a body length and a half of dark water. I knew if I tried to touch bottom, it would be Shasta Lake all over again. Because this activity culminated the lesson, I had nearly an hour to dread before the fact. No matter how hard I prayed, the teachers never forgot this exercise. Beginners or no, we never got a break. The mere mention of steamboating caused me a near panic attack. As the weeks passed, the distance between shore and raft increased. Soon we were unable to make the raft on a single breath–part of the plan, of course. Up bobbed my head for a gulp of air, face back in the water, exhale and flutter kick. My timing was poor; it seemed I always had to share my breath of air with the crest of a wave. It was as if the thing just hovered there waiting for me to bob up and breathe. Then "slap" and I'd be snorting and spluttering, fighting back panic again.

Long before we returned to school, we were already hot and sweaty, longing to be splashing around back at the lake (free swim only, thank you). Then walk to Plemons' service station the town side of the Brewster Bridge to wait for Mom or Margaret Jean Crane to shuttle us home. It was at Plemons' we got our reward for the day's trauma: an ice-cold bottle of pop from the station's chest type pop machine. You put in your quarter, chose your beverage, and scooted the bottle along its metal track through the refrigerated water, and yanked until the machine let go. There in the shade of the station, that ice cold beverage was ambrosia—nothing like a chilled Nehi cherry cola to rinse the lake spume from your mouth.

After another summer or two of Alta swim lessons, we left the steamboating routines in our wakes, advanced enough to learn individual strokes. Our base of operations moved to the big dock a hundred feet offshore. My classmates and I stood dockside where we could study our instructor's technique as she demonstrated the sidestroke, backstroke, treading water (we learned to "scull" using a figure eight motion), the back float, and breaststroke. Then she climbed from the water to critique our form as we swam by her one by one. I was most impressed by the breaststroke, the grace and ease with which the teacher moved through the water, skillfully, beautifully, combining frog kick, arm sweep, and glide. Her arms and legs gleamed ivory against the blue of the lake, her solo performance a fluid ballet of perfection. And to this day, whenever I swim the breaststroke, it is the vision of her, not myself I see gliding through the water.

To reinforce our skills, Mom and Dad took us on a swimming vacation north to Canada. The object was to allow us the opportunity to be around plenty of water and ample time to swim in it. Over the course of the week we swam in the Lakes Osoyoos, Okanogan, and Kamloops. All this swimming exposure helped build stamina and the assurance necessary for us to feel at home in the water.

Lake Osoyoos contributed the most to my swimming skills, my feeling of ease around the water. For several summers we spent a week of Dad's annual two week vacations at the state park in Oroville on the southern end of the lake. Osoyoos had a shallow beach; you could wade from shore a hundred yards before you wet your navel. At the public beach seventy feet offshore, a fifty foot log or plank was anchored parallel to shore. For hours I would swim the length of the plank back and forth perfecting my crawl stroke. Day after day I would swim the plank until I was as relaxed and comfortable as if I were strolling down a city sidewalk. As I swam, I conditioned myself to forget the Shasta experience by repeating the phrase, "The water is my friend," as I glided along the plank. At night in my sleeping bag in the family tent my arms, it seemed, would continue to rise and fall like paddles in the waters of the lake.

In my junior or senior year of high school I used the crawl stroke to swim the length of Alta Lake, the entire mile, from standing flat-footed at the east end until I could touch again at the Whistling Pine Resort in the west. My friend Billy Farley rowed the pilot boat alongside for the hour and a half it took to swim the distance. It was a breezy day, and I swam the entire distance into the wind, against the waves.

Troubled Waters

Even to the advanced swimmer deep waters have their dangers: riptides, undertows, strong, unexpected currents that can sweep away even a strong swimmer in an instant. And those who swim surf and sea are potential shark victims. After I became a swimmer, I can remember only one swim session where I might have been in dangerous waters, may have been in harm's way, though at the time I was totally unaware. Oddly enough, I was on shore high and dry, when the incident happened.

I was ten or eleven when Mom and Dad arranged for Claudia and me to take piano lessons, the intent being to make us as safe and proficient around the keyboard as we were water. They found us a piano teacher, Mr. Gilchrist, a tall, lanky man and bald, a man with large hands and long fingers that could span keys an octave and a half distant on the keyboard. Before I became jaded by the raucous concerts given by those slick-suited, spit shined salesmen who showcase today's mall music stores hawking instruments, I would request Mr. Gilchrist play a lusty rendition of "The Lady of Spain," my favorite organ piece.

Teaching music, I believe, was Mr. Gilchrist's sole support, through which he provided a livelihood for himself, Mrs. Gilchrist, and their two daughters Christine and Susan. Whatever the income was, it was liberal enough for the Gilchrists to own a new Ford Crown Victoria. The Ford had a sunroof, the first I'd ever seen, tinted to protect Mr. G's bald pate from sunburn.

I remember Mrs. Gilchrist as a portly woman, just shy of vivacious. Perhaps at one time she had moved in social circles a cut or two above those Brewster offered: she was always dressed as if she were off to a function. One Fourth of July we invited the Gilchrists to our annual fireworks social, an event less casual than the ranch's summer picnic. Mrs. G. swept in wearing high heels and suit, the skirt so tight the girdle lines showed. Even I could tell her attire was over the top: ours was hardly a country club function.

During the evening's pyrotechnics session, freed from its mooring, a wayward pinwheel took a liking to Mrs. G. and chased her about the place. Giggling and shrieking, she high stepped it across the yard like a drum major, aerating our lawn with each step. Like a heat-seeking missile, the fiery disk matched her zig for zag, as if she had a GPS device in her ample behind. Her exertions snapped a heel. She stumbled and the pinwheel whizzed harmlessly by. It was a night and a performance we'd not soon forget, and though we oohed and aahed our way through the remaining ordnance, it was Mrs. Gilchrist's Independence Day romp that was the grand finale.

During the school year I would leave the school grounds early and walk to Mr. Gilchrist's for my lesson. The lessons continued over the summer. One hot August day in the summer before my seventh grade year—I believe I was his last lesson of the day—Mr. G. asked me if I would like to go swimming in the Methow River some after-noon after the lesson. I had never swum in the Methow before. I had never ridden in a car that had a sunroof either and was up for both adventures. Mr. G. would drive me home. I asked Mom and she consented. The day of the trip I would wear my swim trunks to the lesson.

That August day was a hot one: by the end of the lesson I had puddled the piano bench with perspiration. We drove up the east side of the river three or four miles above Pateros. Mr. Gilchrist parked the Ford, and we walked down the bank across a gravel bar to where a deep pool had formed when the river was at flood. Now, in mid August only a streamlet fed the pool, flowed in above, trick-led out below. Yes, the day was a scorcher, and we had worn only swim trunks and footwear for the walk across the river cobbles and hot sand. We left our shoes on a small sand bar, sprinted across the burning sand to the pool, and dived in.

The water was clear and refreshingly cold. With those long arms and broad hands Mr. G. moved through the water like an aquatic spider monkey. Underwater he was a particularly strong swimmer, his hands scooping aside the water, pulling him through it. He taught me his underwater stroke: extend the arm, pull the hand scoop-like back to your chest and repeat with the other. Mr. Gilchrist demonstrated; I practiced. We swam until I was cold and tired. Then we clambered out and dripped our way to the sand bar to warm ourselves in the sand.

I plopped myself down. Then a strange thing happened. Instead of dropping down beside me, Mr. Gilchrist plopped down behind, scooted up against my back, me snuggled between his outstretched legs, and wrapped his arms around me in a hug. I froze in confusion. No man, even Dad, had ever hugged me like that. I sat immobile with shock as his warm arms pulled me against the barrel of his chest. I wanted to pull away but couldn't. We sat there rocking together in the warm sand, his arms repeatedly clasping and unclasping my cold body. Finally I mustered a "Let's go back in" and pulled free. Back in the pool we swam as before, but once out of the water it seemed he always wanted to grab and hug me. The whole deal made me feel very uncomfortable. Mr. Gilchrist had sat beside me on the piano bench lesson after lesson with not—that I could recall—so much as a pat on the knee. But, come to think of it, Mrs. G. was always somewhere about in the house during the lesson. Now instinct, intuition—some inner voice—warned me something was amiss here along the Methow River: just a boy alone with a man, far away from another soul, another adult.

The rest of the afternoon I spent as much time as possible in the pool, away from those long, grappling arms. Finally I found nerve—or sense—enough to ask to be taken home. I never went swimming with Mr. Gilchrist again.

The incident ended there on the riverbank. I never told Mom or Dad, other family—anyone—about that afternoon. The piano lessons continued as before. There on that sandbar in the late summer sun was the only time I ever felt uncomfortable around Mr. Gilchrist, though I made it a point never to be **that** alone with him ever again.

I replayed the matter of the afternoon later that day, have done so many times since, tried to put a name to his behavior that afternoon, come to terms with my feelings of anxiety and confusion. My family were not huggers, showed affection in ways less physical. Maybe his hugs were innocent; I had simply overreacted. Maybe he clasped me to take the chill of the icy river from my skinny body. Maybe Mr. Gilchrist, father of two daughters, longed for a son to hold in his arms. Maybe.

THE PLAGUE AND I

"Sucks to your ass-mar!"
  the boy Ralph to Piggie in **Lord of the Flies**

Though our move to the river brought adventure and romance, it was not without consequence. I had suffered from asthma nearly from birth, and that first fall on the river my asthma intensified, the attacks more frequent, severe, and prolonged. I believe the onslaught of new allergens, the dusts and pollens which were particularly bad during harvest when the goldenrod and lambs quarter flowered, were in part to blame. These, combined with the stress of a new school, routine, and life, made me wheeze to and from the bus stop, made sleeping at night difficult. I wandered about after school laboring for breath, any vigorous activity impossible. I believe I missed some school that fall, but the asthma eased after the first frosts, and during the winter the attacks subsided. Come spring and a new growing season, however, my asthma returned with a vengeance.

A severe attack would usually last at least three days, sometimes a week, during which time I was bedridden, unable to draw breath, hardly able to struggle downstairs.

Though the upstairs bathroom was only twenty feet from my bed, a one way trip took fifteen minutes. Resting both hands against the wall for support, I would make my way hand over hand toward the bathroom. The effort of three or four steps would exhaust me, and I would pause, panicky, my chest heaving for air. I would return the same way. I had to rest, to sleep sitting upright. After an attack I would feel weak, and my chest would ache for days.

Because of the severity of these bouts, Mom sought medical assistance. Our family physician Dr. Harold Lamberton prescribed a drug called amodrine, little salmon-colored pills that worked on me like a triple shot of espresso. The medication left me nervous, fidgety, and made my heart race. The active ingredient most likely was adrenalin. The amodrine could fend off minor attacks, but nothing seemed to alleviate the big ones. Then it was like my entire ribcage was locked in concrete. When an attack lasted beyond three days, I would visit Dr. Lamberton and be given an injection of aminophylline. Though the drug brought nearly immediate relief, the procedure itself was an ordeal. I was given the drug intravenously, five cc's of it, one cc a minute, five minutes with that needle stuck in the crook of my right arm, pinching away. If I sat during the five minutes, I had a tendency to become lightheaded (twice during the procedure I fainted), and so I lay on my back while the doctor pumped the stuff into my arm. Because the medicines were a temporary fix, only brought relief during an attack, Dr. Lamberton suggested I see an allergist, a nose and throat specialist. Something had to be done, for even commonplace situations could suddenly cause my bronchi to knot shut.

One summer a small circus came to town and set up business adjacent the parking lot behind the open air pavilion where on Saturday nights country boys and cowboys brawled in the fine dust over insults and women to the beat of *The Forty-Niners*, a country swing band from Okanogan. Though the rag tag affair came up two and a half rings shy of a real circus, it caused a stir in our little community, and small crowds of circus goers milled about in the dust on the lookout for the strange and unusual—or any welcome departure from standard rodeo fare.

I recall a somnolent burro or cockle-burred Shetland pony standing hangdog, napping lock-kneed until the random, reluctant child was settled in the swale of its back to be led a quarter's worth of circuits shuffling through the parking lot dust, the child clinging the while desperately to its parent. Horses of any size were commonplace to my experience, and I turned my attention to a crowd gathered before a circular enclosure where a garish sign announced: "See the Giant **HIPPO** Sweat **B**lood!" I had never before seen a live hippo, and one oozing blood would be stellar indeed. I marched to the end of the line and waited.

It was a spectacle I was not destined to see. The dust of the place, plus the pungent aroma of the straw bedding triggered my asthma. Soon I was in the throes of an attack, wheezing and hacking, becoming an attraction myself. Fighting for breath, I had to be taken home. I never saw the hippo. I never saw a single pore trickle blood.

This asthma business was affecting my quality of life, no doubt about it. I had recently joined the Boy Scouts, and the scoutmasters were reluctant to have me along on camping trips for fear I would suffer a bad attack far from civilization. (A mountain environment, I was pleased to discover, kept my asthma episodes at bay.) Also, a schoolmate of mine, Griffin Davies, had chronic asthma so severe his chest cavity was deformed, caved in, from the constant struggle for breath. Griff carried an atomizer everywhere he went and used it constantly. Summers when he went shirtless, Griff's skinny chest was a collapsed bundle of bones, his torso A-shaped, the inverted configuration of the normal torso. I was terrified I also would become deformed, too self-conscious to appear shirtless in public. My asthma attacks, then, could cause deformity, threaten my life. And so Mom made an appointment at the Eye, Ear, Nose, and Throat Clinic in Wenatchee.

Dr. Hilderbrand, the doctor with whom I had the initial conference, suggested immunotherapy to desensitize me against the allergens that triggered the attacks. He recommended I be given a series of skin tests to determine the source of my allergies and scheduled them for the next month. For the tests to be valid, I had to be medication-free for thirty days: no amodrine, no aminophylline, nothing. I remember that month as the most miserable I ever spent on the river. For the entire month my asthma could do with me whatever it would. And that month it showed no mercy. If the drug hiatus would have been scheduled during the school year, I have no doubt I would have missed four weeks of school. Most of the month I was a shut-in and bedridden. I struggled downstairs for meals, labored upstairs back to bed. I may have gone outside a time or two but had little strength or breath to do more than sit on the porch in the sun. Nights in my upstairs bedroom proved nearly unbearable, my labored breathing aggravated by the summer heat. An old electric fan, which reached peak rpm after what seemed like five minutes, clanked away in the dark. Though it did little to move the air, it provided some distraction. I wanted to cry but lacked breath for the effort.

The skin tests were an ordeal of another sort. There I was at the Nose and Throat Clinic, stripped to the waist, prone on an examination table, my back laid out in a grid like one of Dad's orchard charts. The procedure was simple enough. The nurse took a small, screwdriver-like instrument, pressed it into my bare back, and twisted the blade just enough to break the skin. I felt a prick, more like a tickle than anything, with each twist. Row after row, up and down my back until the skin was pricked in a hundred or so places, each scratch numbered in ink. Then the nurse carried in a tray filled with a large assortment of vials containing in emulsion specific molds, grasses, pollens, and foods. On each numbered scratch she squeezed a drop of liquid. The reaction was immediate; my back caught fire. And with each drop the fire spread. Before she finished the tray, my entire back was a rash of hives, one big itch. I fought down the urge to scratch. An attendant measured each welt, rating each on a scale of one to four, smallest to largest, up and down my back. The attendant worked, calling out each measurement while the nurse tallied the results on her clipboard. I heard mostly "threes and fours." The results were a study in hypersensitivity: even the control solution applied to stop the welts from spreading, to quench the fire, caused a reaction. There you had it: I was allergic to the world. Even though the nurse swabbed my back with disinfectant, I was still grinding away on the car seat like a bear with an itch when we arrived in Brewster.

The clinic prepared the serums and sent them by mail, to be administered by syringe and hypodermic needle, a weekly shot in the arm. After a few sessions using an orange as a patient (the skin of an orange supposedly simulates human skin), Mom applied the needle to the sticking place. On shot day I would sterilize the drug paraphernalia in boiling water. Mom would load the syringe with the dosage of the week, and I rolled up my sleeve. As the weeks and months passed I was to become more immune to the allergens, be able to tolerate stronger doses of them. After each shot came a fifteen minute observation period. If my arm swelled, or I developed a wheeze in the first quarter hour, Mom would back off next week's dosage. A vial of adrenaline was kept handy in case I experienced a severe reaction, and although I remember several instances of back peddling the doses, I don't recall anything anaphylactic. Having to mark time for another week was a disappointment: I just wanted the whole ordeal over with.

I accepted the weekly jabs as a fact of life, even gave myself two or three shots in the thigh; I had heard diabetics did this sort of thing, and if they could jab themselves, so could I. The therapy never worked as far as I could tell, and whether we saw the program through to the end or wrote it off as ineffective, I can't remember. I continued to experience bouts of asthma, some severe, all the years I lived on the river. One summer when I was fifteen or sixteen and working fulltime in the orchard, I had an acute attack of the three day variety. The rest of the family had gone on vacation, and I had to fend for myself. Noticing my absence from the crew, Francis came by the house to check on me, called up from the lawn below my bedroom to see if I was still among the living. To some degree immunotherapy did desensitize me: to this day I still experience vestigial numbness in the target area of my right bicep.

I've often wondered what caused my asthma, and why, of all my siblings, I'm the only one still plagued by it. Dad's cigarettes, if not a causative factor, certainly aggravated my condition; on road trips in the car, daily life in the house, second hand smoke always hung in the air. That I was not a breast-fed infant (Mom's theory), according to some disciples of immunology, may have been a factor. At the age of three I developed eczema, thought to be the result of a milk allergy, and thus began my history of allergy and asthma. Perhaps when my genetic die was cast, my lot was snake eyes.

There is a strange irony attached to all this. The chronic disease I've battled all these years may in fact be responsible for my longevity to date. My senior year in high school, before I turned eighteen, I found myself facing the same circumstances as all eighteen year-old American males: registering for the selective service–the draft. As my birthday grew closer, selective service weighed heavily on my peace of mind. In short, I was afraid of the service for the same reason as my peers, I'm sure: the military could be hazardous to your health and longevity. But I do believe–and honestly so–my real fear was basic training. I didn't think I could survive it. To some degree my asthma was activity induced; rigorous exercise could trigger an attack. Dropping and giving them twenty would leave me wheezing on the barracks floor or parade ground. And so I made an appointment with Dr. Lamberton.

In those by-gone days of house calls, Dr. Lamberton had visited my bedside over a period of ten years, sometimes in the late hours of the night, was well aware of my struggles with asthma, had seen me wheeze and gasp for breath in the throes of an attack.

My appointment with him was more than a routine office call; it was a rite of passage in a sense. I was nearly eighteen, would soon graduate from high school, about to leave behind my sheltered life on the riverbank, and according to the old saw, "Go forth and seek my fortune." After the routine exam Dr. Lamberton offered a question and answer session, but I believe it was more a man-to-man talk. It was then Doctor asked me if I had any final questions. I did–the big one, my main reason for the visit. I asked it. "Do you want to go?" I replied that I didn't know if my health would allow it and shared my fears. "I'll send a letter then," he said, shook my hand and said good-bye.

That was the end of it. No draft boards, no selective service physical, no train ride, no boot camp. Later in the summer the result of my visit arrived in the mail: my draft card, selective service status **4F**. Though I was ashamed of the classification, reluctant to share the fact with my friends, I was secretly relieved. I would not have to pit my asthma against the U.S. military, my allergies versus those wool army blankets. Though of no apparent import at the time, there are moments in life that shape one's future, or perhaps in my case guaranteed one. This I believe, and it is not without guilt I say it, but I was spared the horrible cataclysm of the '60's, saved by an afternoon visit and a disease.

Several years later Dr. Lamberton came to my rescue again. He prescribed the bronchodilator *Isoprel* for my asthma. For the first time in my life I could get immediate relief from an attack. It seemed a miracle. Still does. Never again those three day marathon struggles for breath. Gone–and good riddance.

Dam Good Fun

I suppose living on a river whose whims were regulated by hydroelectric dams inspired us to become dam engineers ourselves. In fact, dams were part of our history on the riverbank. We studied them in school, learned about cofferdams, turbines, and turnstocks. We visited them. A late spring outing to Chief Joseph Dam, ten miles upriver, when the spillways disgorged the spring snowmelt, was a special event. Standing at the observation point, you could participate in the power of the spectacle. Nearly at your elbow thousands of metric feet of white water spilled from the massive steel gates, thundered down the spillway, and erupted in boiling geysers a hundred feet below. You stood awestruck in the spray, felt the rumble of the falling water in your feet, legs, entire body. It was a wonderful, horrible spectacle.

Chief Joe Dam, in fact, may have been responsible for my love of puns. My first encounter with a play on words concerned the children whose parents worked for the Army Corps of Engineers, the agency overseeing the construction of Chief Joseph. Local school districts received a government subsidy for the children whose parents belonged to the Corps and had moved to the area to work on the dam. Of course there was the necessary paperwork, which each qualifying child was to have his parents complete and return to school. Our teachers had to remind the procrastinators time and again to return the forms. Mrs. Greaves, my eighth grade teacher, perhaps my most memorable grade school teacher and a character, punned this reminder one day just before dismissal: "All right, you dam people, don't forget your forms tomorrow!" At first my Sunday school sensibilities gave way to shock. I couldn't believe what I'd just heard—and from a teacher, nonetheless. Then I realized the quip was not damnable at all but a clever play on words; they were, after all, "dam" people, weren't they? Come to think of it, Mrs. Greaves loved puns. She had our class perform a minstrel show for the lower grades. I starred in the following exchange:

"Johnny, can you use the word 'fascinate' in a sentence for me?"

"I sho' can. My uncle Joe has ten buttons on his vest, but he is so fat he can only fasten eight."

I wonder why she chose me to be the class punster.

When I was a fifth grader, my class went on a three day environmental field trip, the highlight of which was a tour of Grand Coulee Dam and its powerhouse. Though the massive space that housed the turbines was impressive, I was more amazed at the cleanliness of the powerhouse. The turbines in their freshly painted cowlings sprouted in rows from the polished granite floor like so many German pillboxes. The deliberate hum of machinery was lost in the vastness of the place. We wandered among the mounds of gleaming metal like Lilliputians in Gulliver's machine shop.

The tour wound downward through tunnel-like corridors to the innards of the dam where, I was frightened to learn, we were below water level. We were shown the gleaming steel drive shafts, each more than a foot in diameter, each set in motion by falling water from the lake above and churning through the turnstocks, each spinning away, turning the huge turbines a hundred feet overhead.

Because visiting the bowels of one of the greatest hydroelectric projects on the face of the earth would most likely not happen again, little Judith Spiker brought along her Brownie camera to record the event. Judith was aptly named, a skinny thing–spike-like–with a long, narrow face. Though her little camera was fastened to a strap, Judith, to our entertainment, somehow managed to drop it two or three times. Each time the case hit the granite floor, shards of plastic splintered everywhere. Judith was a fragile child, easily reduced to tears, and the dam burst each time she bounced her camera off the floor. The guide would halt the tour while the teachers comforted Miss Spiker, and we boys exchanged gleeful grins. I don't believe Judith's powerhouse experience ever made it to the photo album; by the time the tour was over, her Brownie was more strap than camera. Her long face sagged onto her chin. I doubt she could have seen much through the viewfinder anyway with her eyes puffed shut.

Thus the inspiration of our own dam building, a summer recreation by which we put to use our own dam experience. In the days before irrigation pipe, rill (ditch) irrigation watered the pear orchard behind our house. Every spring a tractor would drag a ditching machine down the rows, creating the rills that watered the trees through the irrigation season. The orchard sloped enough to allow a gentle flow of water through the ditches, watering the pear trees as it trickled by. An irrigator, knee booted, the ever present shovel balanced on his shoulder, walked the ditches, directing the flow of water, making sure it ran the course of the ditch and not down some gopher hole. The water ran twenty-four hours per ditch, then was diverted to another, then another, until the entire orchard was irrigated. And the cycle then repeated. The water from the rills spilled into a tail ditch at the end of the orchard, flowed down it to the lower side where it pooled and spilled back down the bank. On this tail ditch we built our dams.

The days the tail ditch flowed, we gathered our spades and trowels and marched off to the pear orchard. The orchard soil was sandy loam, the damp earth easy to dig, pack, and move about. Our first engineering task required us to cut a new channel to divert the flow while we built our dam. Then we dammed the ditch and troweled away the dirt behind the dam to form a lake. A spade full of dirt across the new channel redirected the water to the original channel to collect behind the dam. While the lake filled, we patrolled the earthen buffers, watchful for leaks, careful our labors would not be undermined and washed downstream.

When the water pooled to the lip of the dam, our real adventures in hydraulics began. The instant before the water spilled over the lip, we scooped out a section of dam from one side or the other. Propelled by the pressure of the lake, the water burst through the new spillway and exploded downstream. We jogged alongside the flood, followed the wall of water, marveled at the force of the current, its destruction, the washouts and new channels created. When the flow returned to normal, we returned to our project, plugged the hole and repeated the process until we tired of playing in the mud.

We were full of devilish mischief in those days and invited the little kids to join us at the tail ditch for some dam building camaraderie. We, of course, claimed jurisdiction over the headwaters of the ditch, declared the upstream water our engineering district. While our dam stopped the water flow, our little dam building colleagues puttered away downstream, slapping mud pies one upon the other and patting them down until they had the ditch nearly blocked. By this time our dam would have collected a sizeable lake behind it, enough hydraulic evil to purge the ditch of whatever lay downstream. We pulled the plug. The water roared downstream, sliced through whatever mudstrosity the downstreamers had cobbled together. No amount of screams or frantic efforts could stop their project from caving before their eyes, their hour of labor silting away downstream.

A couple of these disasters and the little kids changed their strategy. If their dams were to hold, they would have to make them more substantial, build them faster. And they went at it again in earnest. We countered by dredging and widening our lake, doubling its capacity. One of us would saunter downstream, size up the opposition, and return with news of the competition's latest challenge. If we thought our dam could take theirs, we pulled the plug immediately. If not, we tinkered with water levels and volumes until we were assured victory. Two or three afternoons of seeing their efforts washed downstream, their dam building bubbles burst time and again, the little kids refused to do battle anymore, decided, maybe, their efforts would be more productive exploring the hydraulics of the lawn sprinklers.

With the little kids out of the dam building mix, our penchant for mischief needed new direction. We decided to raise our dam building efforts to new heights. One day when the tail ditch was dry, we dammed the channel with a foot and a half high wall of dirt and proceeded to excavate an extensive pit behind it. Our engineering days on the tail ditch had taught us hydraulics rule number one: the larger the volume of water restrained, the greater the destructive force when it was released. Soon we had dug a hole three feet wide and shoulder depth on my friend Dennis Gragg. As an afterthought we shoveled out steps in the upstream side of the pit, thinking our reservoir might as well double as a swimming hole. After a few adjustments here and there, we stepped back, admired our hole in the ground and waited for the day the tail ditch would run and fill it.

When the water did flow again, there was no hole to greet it. Dad, omnipresent, forever in tune to the pulse of the orchard, discovered our glory hole. Fearing someone might fall in, get hurt, or drown (in the case of a little kid), the orchard road wash away, he ordered out the D2 Cat and had the ol' swimming hole bulldozed and leveled. Shortly after this incident Dad and Francis conspired against us, and soon we found ourselves working summer jobs.

Just a Working Stiff

I think it unfortunate so many young people today lack the opportunity to develop a work ethic, to experience the satisfaction of a tough job done well. I learned about work growing up on the ranch by the river, always had a job, money to save, money to spend. On the Crane Ranch unemployment was unheard of.

Francis Crane believed in work, the values it taught young people, and provided us kids ample opportunity, summers, weekends and after school, to learn its lessons. I guess I've done every kind of job associated with the cultivation of apples, and at least one, to my knowledge, no other worker ever had to do.

To me, then inexperienced in the art of labor, the lesson work taught was basic: I did it; I got paid; I bought stuff–in that order. That's the way work worked. Then I began to see the relationship between work, money, and object was more complex. I realized the authentic Australian boomerang I coveted was not just a miracle stick of wood: it represented x number of hours combing the orchards for the mounds of pocket gophers. That beautifully finished lemonwood bow in the Sears' summer catalog meant I had to hammer and repair piles of apple boxes at two cents a unit before I could become an archer. And a week's worth of hoeing young trees in the dwarf block, where my shirtless body was the only thing that cast a shadow, was what it took for me to explore my musical potential with the five string banjo I longed to pick. In short, I began to understand, on equal terms, both the thing and the labor, the sweat and sore muscles it represented. Not until then did I realize that the value of a material thing included not just the price you paid for it, but the price you paid to get it as well.

But there was more value in work than coin. In my teenage years when Dad and Francis agreed if I were to do a man's work, I should receive a man's wage, I learned work gained me the respect of the men who worked alongside me. These men were intolerant of slackers; I knew for me to be accepted–and I sought their acceptance–I had to work my way into their favor. Though I was "the boss's kid," the last thing I wanted was to be considered one in the derogatory way it so often signified, and I worked extra hard to prove myself, to disprove the slur. I wanted to be known as a hard worker by both the men I worked beside, and my bosses, Dad and Francis, and to prove myself I worked hard. I learned work was about more than money: it was about integrity and pride; it was about respect, my self-worth, the measure of who I was. Work on the riverbank taught me that lesson. And I believe it still.

Blood Money

My early jobs were piece work: the greater the effort, the greater the reward. The first of these required me to be an exterminator: at the age of nine I became a mercenary, a bounty hunter, a scourge of gophers.

The common pocket gopher loved the loosely turned soil of the orchard and the tender roots of the young fruit trees planted there. Named for the furry pouches either side its jaws into which it crammed tuberous delights for transport to the burrow, this subterranean vegematic could turn a budding sapling into a dead stick in just a few short meals. My job was to rid the orchard of these little nippers. Each varmint had a price on its head–or its tail, rather–of twenty-five cents, four to the dollar. During the great gopher epidemic of the mid-fifties, brought on by the interplanting of young trees among the mature, the bounty was upped a dime to fuel our incentive. Then, so to speak, we really made a killing. Proof of dispatch was the stubby inch and a half tail, which we lopped off each victim with our pocket knives and tucked away in a matchbox for safekeeping. We carried the matchboxes in our pockets like coin purses, periodically removing them to tally the contents, crunch a few numbers to compute our earnings. At the end of the month, we would exchange the mummified tails for cash.

The day after pay day, the gopher gang, as we called ourselves, would be on the prowl again, scouring the orchard margins for fresh mounds of earth, telltale signs of gopher activity in the neighborhood. Dad, who knew every foot of orchard on the Crane ranch, would report the location of such activity, and off I'd go, traps in hand, probe in my back pocket and a shovel over my shoulder. We usually ran an eight trap line, enough for four settings, and were discouraged from taking more traps for fear we'd forget a setting and lose them. Also, because gophering was a lucrative trade, a half dozen kids ran trap lines and had to share.

After you located fresh activity, you got down to the business of setting the traps. Using a sharp stick, you probed the ground around the mounds. When the earth gave way suddenly, you knew you had pierced a tunnel. Then you removed two or three shovel loads of earth from the spot, got down on your knees, and jabbed the sides of the hole until your fingers caved in the tunnel. With your hand you hollowed out the mouths of each opening–twice because the tunnel was cut in half–enlarging it wide and deep enough to insert a trap in each portal.

Now that I think back on it, the gopher trap was a vicious device, so designed that each gopher died a horrible, lingering death. Today, animal rights groups protest against just such traps. They were about eight inches long–gopher length–made of heavy wire. Two sharpened prongs crossing each other **X** fashion when unset, did the dirty work. The prong arms ended in a coiled spring, allowing the prongs to snap together when released. You set the traps by pressing down both prong arms with your thumb. Then you held them in the open position with the trip lever, the end of which you inserted in the metal trip plate. You adjusted the sensitivity of the trap by pulling the trip plate gently forward until the tip of the lever barely protruded from the hole in the plate. Carefully, you slid a trap into each entrance and covered the hollow with a chunk of sod to block out any daylight that might tip your bounty hunter's hand. From each trap dangled a bailing wire tether a foot and a half long, one end of which was fastened to the spring end of the trap, the other a loop you used to carry the traps on your rounds. Before you left each set, you ran a stick through each loop and shoved it firmly into the ground to prevent a trapped animal from dragging his wounded body and the trap deep into the run out of reach. When the last trap was set, you went home and left the traps to work their evil.

The next day I would pocket my knife and matchbox and walk the trapline. At each set I would remove the sod plug and drag out the traps. Almost always there was carnage. Sometime during the night, as I slept the sleep of angels, the hungry gopher, in search of the succulent root, clambered across an obstruction in his run, pushed against it, and the next moment was impaled through the bowels, helpless to do anything but die.

No doubt my bounty hunter days would have been short lived if I replayed the previous scenario each time I yanked a stiff victim from its tomb. But those were cruel times, and I had a matchbox to fill, a piggy bank to feed. I would shake the stiffened carcass from the blood-clotted prongs, slice off the tail for the matchbox, reset the trap for the unsuspecting mate or offspring, and head for the next set.

I was not always a passive participant in gopher death. Sometimes I pulled a trap only to discover a struggling victim, which I would have to dispatch with a quick whack to the head with a stick of apple wood. After the *coup de grace* I would close my eyes quickly in attempt to blink away my murderous act. Though it happened infrequently, I might pull the wire tether and nothing budged, a sign I'd come up empty, was tugging at a dry hole. The gopher had sensed something amiss, buried and sprung the trap. I remember at least one cunning gopher that for one week running buried my traps. In frustration I pulled up stakes and left him to work his mischief on one of my colleagues.

Once I pulled a trap and to my surprise found a snarling, snapping weasel fast in its grip. Apparently it had gone gophering and ended up the victim itself. Crazed by pain and fear, the weasel slashed at the trap, its teeth chattering against the trip plate. I was frantic to kill it, put to rest its pain, its frenzied champing. It was defiant even in death, jaws locked on the trip plate, legs grasping the trap. I turned away, weak in the knees until I knew its quivering, proud body was still.

It was not noble work, my first job, dealing out pain and death, but I pocketed my money at the end of the month and continued to tend a trap line for two or three years. One month I hit a gold mine in the homeplace pears and turned in nearly forty dollars worth of tails, with help from Dad, who tended my trap line while I was bedridden with a siege of spring asthma.

Two Cents a Box

I have previously mentioned the importance of the wooden apple box in the harvesting of fruit. To contain and transport pears and apples from the field required thousands of boxes. During harvest these were shuttled from orchard to camp, emptied and returned to field again to be refilled. In the off season the boxes were stacked in nests of three, eight nests high in mountainous piles, in numbers twenty thousand strong. The frequent handling of the boxes, plus the fact they were always exposed to the elements, the rains of spring and fall, winter snows, and scorching summer sun mandated each undergo annual maintenance. A perfect job for a kid. So for the next couple of summers I spent considerable time parked alongside a vast pile of boxes, getting to know each up close and personal.

Francis Crane himself conducted job orientation, careful to emphasize time and again, the importance of our work. We exchanged grins of satisfaction, as if we ourselves were God's chosen. When Francis finished, those of us handpicked for the job were assigned a box pile of work and turned loose to become hammering men. Box repair was piece work, the going scale two cents a box, plus all the slivers you could pull. As I soon discovered, the job was unpleasant at best, but at least it was honest work, the pay not tainted by the blood of little animals.

The task was basic: prepare each box in the pile for the coming harvest. Our tools: a box hatchet, nail machine, workbench and cast iron bracket to steady and secure the box. Designed especially for the job, the box hatchet was both ax and hammer, one end a square striking surface grooved with teeth like a meat tenderizer to "grab" the head of each nail, the other a blade, notched for pulling nails, to pry or split away a side or bottom. The nail machine was a three level affair: the lower level a trough for holding nails, which you dusted with lime for easier handling; midlevel, three wire tracks to dispense the nails; top level, a tin chute down which the nails slid to the tracks. You grabbed a handful of nails from the nail basket, dropped them into the chute where they cascaded into the tracks and dangled until needed. The machine aligned the nails so you could remove them four or five at a time and set each quickly, rapid fire, machine gun style. Slightly larger than the box itself, the cast iron bracket steadied each box while you made repairs.

We were also supplied bundles of sides and bottoms with which to replace the broken or damaged pieces. One whack of the hatchet against the bailing wire strap and a bundle would pop open, releasing pockets of fresh sawdust and a fragrance of new cut pine. The bottoms were of a different construction, not solid pieces like the sides, but three thin slats for give to reduce bruising, cleated together with staples on each end. To prevent the cleats from splitting, we soaked the bottoms in a fifty gallon drum of water. A crude tent, a tarp draped and nailed to a square two-by-four frame held aloft by four orchard props, complemented our workspace. Though they were meant to screen the sun, we baked beneath them in the heat of the day, our noses assaulted by the oily stench of tarpaulin. These shades had the annoying tendency of taking flight during the winds of occasional thunderstorms, landing inverted some distance away, legs askew. Work would have to wait while we re-erected our tents over the workbench where they canted tentatively, guaranteed to relocate again during the next storm, almost as if they too deplored the monotony of the place.

Tackling the huge piles of boxes was overwhelming—one kid armed only with a box hatchet versus twenty thousand wooden boxes, each in some state of disrepair, each a project in itself. You first examined the box for "shiners," wayward nails whose tips protruded from the wood. A shiner inside a box could gouge the fruit, which would have to be discarded or culled. An exterior shiner could gash a worker's hand. All shiners had to go. If you fudged the job, pounded the offending nail flush with the wood, you were sure to be discovered during one of the periodic inspections by a crew boss, Dad, or perhaps even Francis. You then were required to retrace the last couple days' work, retooling each box again, this time for free. No, each shiner had to be extracted from the box. You would pry the nail away from the wood with your hatchet until you could free it enough to slip the notch under the head and yank the offender free. Often the head would snap, and there you were, the nail shining away and no means to remove it. Then you would have to gouge the contentious metal out with the hatchet blade. The most challenging shiner was the one whose head lay under a side or bottom, (no thanks to a former repairman), no other way to get at it but to remove the entire piece. Extracting a difficult shiner could take considerable sweat, perhaps a few tears, and fifteen or twenty minutes—all to put two more cents in your pocket.

If a box were shiner-free, you inspected the first side for loose nails. Weathering caused the pine boards to warp and lift the nails. You reset the old nails with a new one alongside. If the side was split or caved in, you replaced it with a gleaming fresh one from a bundle. Then you flipped the box in the bracket to inspect the bottom. Replacing a bottom was where you earned your money. You could remove a side easily by tapping upwards from the inside. A bottom, however, had to be splintered apart with the hatchet to reveal enough nail head to get a purchase. (Seemed strange that most shiners lurked beneath the bottom cleats.) On to the last side, and then to metal rollers where you shoved the box along with the rest of the day's work. Sometimes a box required only nail setting, thus an easy two cents, but with most, your pay came dearly. When the rolls would hold no more, you tallied your boxes, nested them in threes and stacked each nest neatly in the repaired pile, which as the days passed, seemed to grow ever so slowly, overshadowed always by that looming mountain that bristled with shiners and stove in bottoms.

The box pile was dirty, miserable work. I hated it. Mold grew on the boxes and the musty smell commingling with the pungent tarp brought the old telltale tickle to my throat, coaxed a wheeze from my lungs. What I hated most was the tedium of the work, knowing I was expected to transfer that mountain of a pile one box at a time in good repair to a new pile by summer's end. And I hated being alone, stuck out there in the middle of the orchard, in the dusty heat of the day with nothing to keep me company but my bottle of Kool-aid. I welcomed any diversion. A red-tailed hawk on motionless pinions, carried high by the heat of the valley, spiraling itself into a speck. The occasional weed-laden dust devil, passing through, rattling my tent, filling the air with dust and litter, cooling my sweating body. Sometimes an orchard vehicle, a tractor, truck, or Dad's Jeep passed by. To me it was a parade. Out of sheer boredom I took a handful of nails and hammered the initials **TJ** into my work bench. The hours to lunch, to five o'clock, seemed interminable. Mom suggested I set a quota of two hundred boxes a day, four bucks wages, and then rest from my labors, steel myself for the next day's two hundred more. Though the quota gave me purpose, the rolls filled oh so slowly, the shiners more troublesome, that hammer heavier with every swing.

While it seemed my box pile loomed as large as ever, the other kids' dwindled. As the summer wound down, I remember being asked if I thought I could finish my pile. Then my pride became an issue: did I want to be the only kid unable to finish his pile, the boss's kid not up to the job? I was ambivalent about this: on the one hand, my reputation was on the line—was I man enough to finish the job; on the other, maybe the first kid to finish his pile would move to mine, help me out, keep me company. At this point in the ordeal, I believe I would have paid my entire summer earnings to anyone willing to step forward and take my hatchet. I don't recall if I finished the job, nor do I remember any celebration to mark the event, if a fuss were made, if at the soda fountain at Day's Drugstore I set up strawberry sodas all around for my fellow box repairmen.

One session at the box pile was anything but tedious, one of my first sessions, when the job still had allure. I had only a few hours experience on the job. In fact, it might have been my first day at the box pile. After dinner one evening in May, I thought I would hammer out a few cents' worth at my box pile in the neck of the 80. The irrigation season had just begun, and Dad needed to make his rounds to check the sprinkler systems. He said he'd be somewhere in the area, would drop by later to see how I was doing. Dad drove us to the neck in the Jeep, transporting my bicycle in case I wanted to leave before he was ready.

I hammered away at a few boxes, satisfied with the job, pleased with my progress, proud of myself. I pulled a box with a broken side and set to work to replace it with a new one. The loose nails pulled easily, but some still held fast. I would have to dislodge the board by knocking loose the remaining nails. Using the hammer end of the hatchet, and guiding the hammer along the side, I struck the inner surface of the board. The nails would not give. Holding the box firmly with my left hand, I stepped back a foot or more for leverage and swung from the waist. Night fell instantly, fret with sparklets that burst, then faded and winked out. What had happened? I shook my head to clear the confusion. I stared at the box. The broken side was intact as before. The board had not stopped the blow, but my forehead had. I had misjudged my swing and missed the box. I couldn't believe I'd done such a clumsy thing. I returned to work, hammering more cautiously.

The evening was mild, even a bit cool, and I had not been long on the job. With the back of my hand I wiped away the moisture from my eyebrows. Odd indeed to be sweating, I thought. The back of my hand and forearm came away red. Blood, lots of it. Bright red, now dripping from my brow, off my nose. I did not know then that the slightest head wound leaked enough blood to make one appear the victim of an ax murderer. The blood coursed down my face. As if my forehead were a beef steak, the little hammering teeth had neatly perforated it. I panicked, and at this point in the narrative I think it appropriate to say I screamed bloody murder. I bellowed out, "Help!" I bellowed for Dad, "Dad! Help!"

All my commotion brought Dad on the run. He must have panicked too, seeing before him a howling kid–his kid–face a river of blood, still clinging to the weapon he had raised against himself. I believe Dad panicked, either forgot about the Jeep or abandoned it for transportation closer at hand because the next thing I remember we had careened through the orchard to the county road, me bouncing and jostling around on the handlebars of my bike. Dad, my two-wheeled ambulance driver, churned away at the pedals, his kneecaps occasionally lifting my behind an inch or two off the bars. My wound clotted long before we arrived home, probably congealed from the wind rush in my face. At home a washcloth removed the gore, and a band-Aid repaired the wound, which faded into a scar just below the hairline I had at that age. The incident left me wondering if I would ever work a ranch job that involved no blood.

A Rare Perfume

When I was twelve or thirteen, I left piece work to the younger kids, began working for hourly wages, and officially became a hired hand. I first drew hourly wages moving waterlines in the new planting known as the "11," a sagebrush flat where a much younger Dennis Gragg and I scavenged for scorpions among piles of rotted boards. (I was stung by one of these little arachnids when Dennis, stooping to capture another, tipped his coffee can, spilling a half dozen irate captives on my bare arm. At the clinic I was relieved to learn I was not a goner. Dr. Stout informed Mom my little segmented assailant was far less venomous than its bigger Southwest cousins, that I was more likely to die from a bee sting instead, and to go home and put ice on the sting.)

Sixty-five cents an hour: my wages for moving irrigation pipe twice a day back and forth across the eleven acre block of Red Jonathons. By my mid teens I was drawing top wages, a dollar ten an hour, ten hours a day, seven days a week two weeks on end, dragging a hundred foot spray hose through acres of orchard alongside seasoned regulars. During harvest the workdays lengthened to eighteen, sometimes twenty hours. Afraid I'd fall asleep if I stopped moving—especially mid-ramp, wheeling a handtruck full of packed fruit—I consumed No-Doz pills as if they were aspirin. But I was making harvest wages, $1.25 an hour, top dollar—and eligible for the harvest bonus to boot—those days of two cents a box long gone.

Careful not to foster the stigma of "the bosses' kids," Dad and Francis closely monitored our progress up the ladder of ranch labor. I'm certain considerable thought and discussion preceded any new job we were given. Could we measure up? How would the crew react? Would they consider us heirs of privilege, freeloaders on the gravy train? The Crane boys felt the pressure. I know I did. Francis and Dad wanted us to be workers, understand what it was to serve up a hard day's work. And we wanted to be known as hard workers. Like all those in supervisory capacity, our fathers, I'm sure, were keenly aware of the adversarial relationship between worker and boss, labor and management. I believe Dad and Francis—the term for it in today's workplace—micromanaged us kids, knowing it was better for us—and them—to be treated as labor ourselves.

Whenever I worked among the crew, I felt keenly my loyalties were divided, always tested. I wanted to be accepted as an equal by the regulars. This meant turning a deaf ear to disparaging remarks made about "Johnny." Coming to Dad's defense was sure to mark me as "the boss's kid," lose me the trust and respect I craved from the crew. Francis was a different matter: after all, he was Dad's boss too, and I was quick to side with crew sentiment in his censure. (Once I apparently translated my dissatisfaction into gesture, which Francis saw and later made the topic of a dialogue about my attitude.) Whenever a crew member vilified Dad, I hurt because he was my dad; I hurt because I was his son. But I shouldered the hurt, suppressed it because I was one of the crew.

Where I was concerned, it seemed Dad always worked hard at not showing favoritism. I felt he was always looking over my shoulder, watching like Big Brother. I would work non-stop nearly all day at the hardest job without once seeing him. But let me take a minute's break, no sooner had I eased my exhausted rear end to the deck than Dad would step out from behind a tree and make me feel as if I had been dogging it all day. Dad, I thought, was master of the conditional "but." No matter what job it was, I was doing it "well"–**BUT** there was always something more I could do to improve. To me, it was a "but" that decried mediocrity. Ours was the traditional battle of father/son, the eternal issue of the son trying to measure up.

Looking back across all those years, I know it must have been equally difficult for Dad to balance the roles of boss and father, careful not to let it appear he was favoring me over the other workers. Perhaps that's why Dad assigned me a job I'm sure would have had the staunchest of my co-workers quit the ranch in disgust.

Above the 80 planting, the Red Bartlett block was situated on a sloping hill in shallow, sandy soil. Beneath the pears lay a shelf of bedrock, probably granite. The porous earth allowed the irrigation water to filtrate quickly to the bedrock substrata, where directed by the sloping hardpan, it flowed downhill into the lower orchard. Here the water pooled on the level ground, creating a marsh among the fruit trees. These trees were sickly, their foliage yellow, "feet" always wet from too much irrigation. In attempt to drain the area, the crew buried a six inch galvanized pipeline through the marsh, directing the seepage across the soggy area to drain away downhill. Though far from a perfect solution, the drain kept the area dry enough to prevent the trees from drowning. One day, however, Dad noticed the telltale jaundiced hue had returned to the leaves on a dozen trees in the boggy flat. Dad inspected the drain. It was plugged, the water backed up: the marsh had returned. Dad assigned me to fix the problem.

The tree roots were the problem, Dad seemed to think, had split the pipe and massed there, obstructing the drain. This seemed logical to me. I had to find where the obstruction lay, then remove it. I snaked a hundred foot plumber's tape down the drain, shoved it along until it would slide no further and marked the steel tape where it entered the pipe. I removed the tape, stretched it along the ground above the buried line, and drove a stake above where I believed the blockage lay. I dug a two foot pit at the spot, shoveled away until I struck the pipe, and cleared enough space around it to operate. A few minutes with a hammer and cold chisel, and I had chiseled a jagged foot long incision. Carefully, so as not to gash my hands, I pried apart the split pipe. Immediately the pit filled with water past my elbows. Whatever clogged the pipe was close at hand. Tentatively I slid my hand into the orifice, searching for the blockage, expecting my fingers to close on a fibrous mass of roots. Instead, they closed on a furry snout and teeth. I jerked my hand free as if I'd been bitten. The tragic story of that pointed little snout lingered on my fingertips. Some unfortunate skunk had somehow spelunkered down the pipe, wedged itself in there, and drowned.

(This was not my first encounter with a skunk that had stuck its head where it didn't belong. While moving water lines one morning I heard a "clink-clink" from the roadside ditch, went to investigate, and discovered a skunk, its head held captive by a jelly jar. Apparently it had visited the camp dump, found the jar, and wishing to get at the sticky remnants, became stuck itself. I wanted to do it a kindness, release it, but was afraid of how it might receive my charity. The skunk-in-a-bottle clunked its way across the county road into the sagebrush, down into the canyon. I never learned its fate.)

Because the skunk no longer seemed a threat—or so I thought—this time I slipped both hands into the dark passage, firmly grasped the furry skull, and as if assisting in a stillbirth, tried to coax the corpse from its watery tomb. The skunk held fast, turgid in rigor mortis, swollen to the sides of the pipe. A breech delivery, I decided, was my next option. I moved to the back of the pit and went to work on the skunk's posterior. Once more into the breech. I grasped the tail. The carcass may have been there for weeks, kept fairly well-preserved by the cold water, but when I yanked the tail, the hide came away in my hands slicker than skin off a scalded tomato. At this effort the musk glands burst, spilling their putrid contents, which like oil quickly rose to the surface, coating both my arms with a green film. What foul obstetrics this was! The stench was even too much for my dog Tiny, whose personal covenant it was to investigate every skunk in the county, and though usually he was my companion on the job, now turned fickle, left the **O.R.** and slunk away to the orchard road for a breath of fresh air.

I removed the corpse caesarian section, surrounded, it seemed, by a green haze. The pit and pipe emptied quickly, draining away everything but the stink. I would return the next day for closure after the site had had a good night's airing, but until then I sought out less pungent environs. No one had much to do with me the rest of the day. At home I was allowed quick access to my swim trunks and for an hour or so my only companions were the river and a bar of soap. After the soap dissolved (or **was** dissolved), the primary effluvia washed downstream, I returned home, drew a hot bath, and went to work on the secondary layers. Before I turned in for the night, I sprayed half a can of room deodorant into my pajamas. I drifted off to sleep amid a medley of olfactory stimulation. But when you're the boss's kid, you do what you have to do.

ASSHOLES WITH HATS

Besides the regulars who lived and worked on the ranch for years, a variety of men drifted into camp, our lives, and then disappeared on down the road, never to be seen or heard of again. Even Jesus worked on the ranch one harvest—or so I thought. In those days a communal mailbox, an apple box nailed to the side of the cookhouse, served the ranch. On my way home from the bus stop, I would shuffle through the box, gather the family mail, and carry it home. One day during harvest I checked the mail and was astonished to find a letter addressed to Jesus. "Jesus, here on the ranch!" I thought. A vision of the Savior, Our Lord, picking bucket strapped to his Holy shoulders, making a radiant descent to the world of men down a twelve foot orchard ladder played in my head for a moment. Flushed with excitement, I rushed home with news that the ranch had been chosen as the site of the Second Coming. I was disappointed to learn the article of mail was addressed to one of the seasonal Hispanic workers the ranch ferried north each fall to help with harvest. What I thought Messianic was not an Holy Epistle after all but a secular message more likely dictating where and when to send the check.

I once read a story about an Irishman who came home drunk from the bars and was asked by his wife to attend their infant son. The father lifted the child from the crib by its diaper. Perhaps too much drink made the man careless. Perhaps the diaper was loosely bound, but the infant slipped from it, and the father's grasp, fell head-first to the floor. The fall crushed the child's skull; it died instantly. Haunted by his son's death and his part in it, the distraught man abandoned his wife and family and became a transient, a derelict of the streets, a bum and a drunk.

I tell this story by way of explanation, for each of the drift-ers who came to camp, drew wages for a week or season and then moved on, perhaps had a similar story, some cataclysmic event that uncoupled him from mainstream humanity and set him adrift down the alleys of the world. This story we did not learn, nor was it ever shared. Willard Lowrance, one of the camp's regulars, called these vagrants "assholes with hats." Lowrance did not use the word in the pejorative sense of today's lexicon but as a matter-of-fact assess-ment of their lives, their detachment from the world of common human endeavor: no solid niche of their own design, no home, fam-ily, goals, dreams. They seemed to live their lives in the shade of their own hats, a gray people adrift in the world like thistledown. They were workers, no doubt about that, invaluable to the harvest. While some lasted the season, others, after three or four days' work drew their pay, put harvest on hold, shuffled off and invested their wages in Mogan David or Old Smiley fortified wine and a three day binge. For the most part these men were all rough edges, their talk profane and blasphemous, their stories ribald and salty, the constants in their lives liquor and Saturday nights. But without these "apple knockers," the fruit would have rotted on the trees. In sum, they were a fascination to us.

Homer Helm, the home place irrigator, wintered in Arkansas. Perhaps I should have mentioned earlier that Homer was another harbinger of spring. He arrived by bus, simultaneously, it seemed, with the annual priming of the home place pump, ready for the summer's rill detail. I have no idea how many years Homer had worked the ranch before my family came, but he was already an old man in his sixties when I knew him. Homer could have been the prototype for the "old geezer." Irascible and crusty, we never knew if his mood was fair or foul, thus a meeting with him was certain to be a surprise. Homer delighted in salacious talk, sexual innuendo, and friendly banter with the young men in camp about their exploits between the sheets. I remember old Homer, in his southern Arkie drawl, counseling a young member of the crew, a newlywed, about matters of the bedroom, advising the young man he might for variety, "Lay her [the new bride] on the kitchen table and pull her on like an old boot." Then he laughed his lecherous old geezer laugh.

Homer was as wizened as the Old Dead Tree, all old bones draped with a skin mottled and freckled with liver spots. Even with his shovel and mud-caked rubber boots I doubt he'd have nudged the scale at a hundred pounds. Homer wore wire-rimmed glasses anchored firmly to a pair of paddle-like ears. As he walked the ditches, his irrigator's shovel at rest on his right shoulder, he seemed to list a bit, appeared from a distance to have two ears to starboard.

Throughout the irrigation season, Homer stalked the home place apples and pears, turning spigots on and off, channeling water from one ditch to the next, making sure the water ran the course of the ditch, didn't meander off course and trickle down a gopher hole somewhere. Twenty or thirty acres of orchard were his jurisdiction. It was Homer, I'm sure, who tipped our hand, told Dad about our elaborate tail ditch excavation. He knew his job and did it well.

Each spring Francis and Dad speculated if Homer would return for another season. One spring he was ill and came late. The same summer while he was helping shorten a section of pipe from the pump intake line and raise the pump house above the rising river, Homer slipped on the wet rocks. He went down hard across a steel rail of the pump house tracks and cracked several ribs in the fall. After Homer returned from the hospital, he removed his shirt and showed the concerned crew his injury. His ribcage had been taped and bound to prevent movement and allow the bones to knit. I was there to see the sight and couldn't help but think how much Homer's naked torso looked like the racks of ribs on display at the butcher's shop. Homer convalesced and finished out the season, his last on the river. He returned to Arkansas that fall. We never heard from him again.

"Pee Wee," the crew called him, although his checks were made out to a Clarence Clutter, came to the ranch after a hitch in the merchant marine. Aptly named, Mr. Clutter no doubt could walk through ships' bulkheads, his sailor's hat still riding high on his crown. I delighted in the alliterative name–Clarence Clutter–his only claim to the poetic, and the anchor tattoo on his forearm. I had never seen a tattoo before. To me, Pee Wee's anchor represented the exotic, down to the sea in ships, foreign shores far beyond my riverbank. On cool days or in bad weather, Clutter went about his work wrapped in a service-issue pea jacket. The color of smoke, Pee Wee kept his hair cropped short, military style. Whether by his own barbering or a skin condition, the man's stubbled skull appeared a patchwork, like the hide of a mangy hound. In pensive moments when he paused at work or leaned on a shovel, Pee Wee would work his mouth and lips in an odd manner, almost as if his lower lip was playing with the upper. In these moments he worked his mouth as if something was loose in there, some foreign object, perhaps a bone chip he sought to extract with his tongue. Maybe he was just adjusting his dentures.

Clutter had a peculiarity of speech, a penchant for redundancy when the conversation required emphasis. In these situations, Pee

Wee would issue a statement, usually terse, and immediately echo it: "That's what I told him! That's exactly what I told him!" A cloudiness of spirit cast a pall over Pee Wee's work days, his life; he was a dingy little cynic, a camp Eeyore. When an official at the Social Security office told Pee Wee he had to present a birth certificate before he could apply for benefits, he angrily replied (in duplicate): "I must have been born—I'm here. I must have been born—I'm here, ain't I!" His recounting the incident gave us all a good laugh, though I'm certain the clerks at Social Security appreciated neither his humor, his logic—nor the echo. Clarence Clutter retired from orchard work and left the ranch. I'll vouch for the fact he was still very much alive when he departed.

One of Dad's favorite transients was George Roenfranz, an ex-prizefighter. Dad followed the sport of boxing and I know George impressed him. Roenfranz had the squat center of gravity of a master of the ring. It must have taken something to knock him from his feet. His big, muscled arms stood out from his torso. According to Dad, George looked like "he could handle himself," no doubt must have sent a man or two down for the count. It was obvious George had taken a blow or two himself. A silly putty nose pasted in the middle of his face and mashed to one side testified many a sharp jab had landed. George's ears were gnarled cartilage. When he talked, his voice traveled over gravel: his larynx had taken a licking too. Odd, I thought, because George had almost no neck. His head seemed to sprout from his shoulders. I doubt any amount of battering could have extinguished the life in his eyes, which twinkled blue beneath the widow's peak hairline that spread a blonde crewcut across his crown. George worked for Cranes just one summer. I thought it strange the meaty hands grasping the handles of the push mower were once gloved fists delivering blow after punishing blow to head and body, the feet now plodding one after the other through new-mown grass had once carried a bobbing, weaving boxer about a canvas ring. George likely thought it strange too.

Most of the crew did not own transportation. They arrived in town by bus, either took the town taxi to the ranch or walked the five mile stretch. Since the cookhouse provided meals, there was little need to make a trip to town during the week. When the crew numbers swelled as they did during thinning season or harvest, a bus or truck would shuttle the men to town on Saturday afternoons so they could pick out whatever essentials they needed for the week ahead, and, of course, sample the wares at the local watering holes. The return trip was up to them. By Sunday afternoon most were back in their bunkhouses recuperating from the night before, ready for another week's work.

The crew did not own cars because they could never set aside money enough to buy them. Or perhaps they knew better. Consider the case of Howard Kessner. Kessner had his own car, drove to the ranch one summer and hired on to thin apples. He was an older man, in his late sixties, a confirmed drunk and proved it one Saturday night after an evening of bellying up to the bar. On the drive home Howard failed to negotiate the curve at the "ll" where the county road swept hard left uphill. His car plunged down a seventy-five foot embankment into the canyon. I say Kessner failed to negotiate the turn, but more likely the fellow was so intoxicated he never attempted to steer the vehicle or blacked out moments before it left the road. Next morning irrigators discovered the car, went to investigate, and found Howard on the floorboards of the wreck, still drunk and sleeping it off but otherwise unscathed—a miracle in those pre-seat belt days. The liquor had apparently cushioned his fall.

While Kessner's story was the talk of the camp for a week or so, another story was his undoing. One evening after work the old man approached two or three little girls who were playing a game with a pile of recently thinned green apples. He asked the girls if they would like to see a magic trick: he would make an apple disappear then reappear. The girls were curious. Of course they would. Howard asked one to select an apple for the demonstration. He then took the apple and made it disappear by dropping it down the top of the girl's dress. The apple reappeared when the old man reached under her dress and retrieved it. Apparently Howard performed this sleight-of-hand a time or two with the other girls as well. One of them saw right through Howard's magic trick, didn't appreciate the hands on portion of the audience participation role, and told her parents. The incident was reported to Francis who fired the camp magician on the spot, told Kessner to draw his wages and hit the road before he summoned the county sheriff. Today, Kessner's perverted prestidigitation would have landed him in jail for sure, and I wonder at the wisdom of loosing the old scoundrel to work his depraved magic on other young audiences somewhere else on down the road.

A pair of ranch characters were amateur archaeologists, though I'm sure they never considered themselves as such. In an earlier time Indians followed the river during their annual migrations to their hunting grounds, camped along its banks, and these old encampments produced artifacts: arrowheads, spear points, scrapers, beads, pottery shards, either discarded or left behind. Gordon Hice and Kenny Sage spent their weekends combing these old sites, gathering and collecting the flint and obsidian history of the area.

Gordie Hice was a squat runt of a fellow, with swine-like features, sandy eyelashes and the close set eyes of a hog. His bristle-cut hair and ruddy complexioned face complemented the porcine image. He had a narrow gash of a mouth, a miniature orifice that looked to little purpose, but shove a harmonica between his lips, and Gordie could make it wail, make it weep, the notes curling and weaving through the stubby, plump fingers. The sandy lashes would fall, and Gordie would be in rapture, his roly-poly body swaying to "Red Wing" or "The Irish Washerwoman," his favorite. I bought a harmonica, carried it with me everywhere I went, played it every chance I got. Oh, but I wanted to play the mouth harp like Gordie!

Kenny Sage, the other half of this strange duo, played Jeff to Gordie's Mutt. Kenny was a young fellow in his early thirties. He had the build of a catcher, a stolid body, the physical toughness of a Thurman Munson, though he lacked the Yankee's tenacity of mind and spirit. Kenny had an unique laugh, a guttural bray that would choke you if you tried to mimic it. He would laugh abruptly in mid conversation, leaving you to retrace the thread of it, wonder where the humor was. Perhaps Kenny had a quirky sense of humor; perhaps the humor came from within, some internal comedic monologue; perhaps the joke was on him. Who knew?

To Ken, the measure of a man was his sexual prowess; one yardstick (a rather bold term in this context) in his paradigm of masculinity was the abundance of ejaculate a man could produce during sexual climax: the more juice, the greater the man. No doubt Kenny met his own standards, probably surpassed them.

Once I happened across Kenny along the county road just above the Brewster Bridge. Ken owned a little car, an Isetta 3000. This little joke of a car had only one door, which doubled as the vehicle's front end. You opened it, and out swung steering wheel and all. The little car had broken down—a flat tire, or given Kenny's female passenger—a broken axle. The woman would have made two of Kenny. She was a Class-A floozy, and, delicately put, snot-slinging drunk. Ken's doubled date was giggling hysterically, not the least upset by her predicament, hardly the typical damsel in distress. She was obviously along for another kind of ride. I could offer no help, left the two standing by the Isetta in the midst of the road and their laughter like two circus clowns performing the tiny car act. To tackle such a woman in a car that small—well, that was the measure of a man.

Kenny was not without other talents. His fascination with Indian artifacts led him to study and learn the art of crafting stone tools. He became so accomplished it was difficult to distinguish his arrowheads and spear points from those Indian toolmakers produced centuries earlier. Kenny would chip away at a chunk of bottle glass and in mere minutes produce an arrow tip of museum quality. He once gave me a spear point chipped from a beer bottle, translucent, perfectly symmetrical. If I hadn't dropped the piece and broken it, it might have passed for jewelry.

Tired of screening tons of sand for artifacts, Gordie and Ken took their archaeology out of bounds, decided to shift their archeological digs from the riverbank to a remote burial ground somewhere on the Colville Indian Reservation. Among other artifacts of desecration, they carried away two human skulls, (or so they bragged; I never did see them). They named the skulls Hezekiah and Ephraim, Mormon names, adding insult to desecration. And wherever they kept their collection, these macabre bones kept vigil over the secret horde.

Both men ran afoul of tragedy. Gordon Hice took his life; Kenny Sage married. Gordie succumbed to the demons of alcohol and depression and a pistol shot to the head. Kenny married a homely, near-sighted girl named Gladys, even then pregnant with his child. For a while they lived on the ranch in pickers' cabins. I felt sorry for the plain, big bellied girl. She seemed eternally pregnant, always about to give birth. I sympathized with her too because her husband had demons of his own. Perhaps he was besieged by the restless spirits of two red men. I don't know—but something stilled his laughter. More often at work we saw him pause, stare trance-like and vacant into space, and we knew the demons were with him. Kenny could not sleep nights. It was discovered he kept a loaded .45 beneath his pillow. Gladys, fearing for her life and the unborn child's, left the ranch to live with relatives. Kenny left the ranch, too—or was taken away—to the mental hospital at Medical Lake. I never learned his fate. I wonder what became of the two skull sentinels and the collection of Indian artifacts. I wonder if Gladys ever had her child.

After work and supper, after the men left the cookhouse, and by twos and threes filed back to their cabins, after quiet settled golden on the evening, I would return to camp and visit with the ranch denizens. Fred Walters was one of my favorites. Walters was a handsome man, nearly always clean shaven and well-groomed, his thick raven hair oiled and neatly combed. Fred, like most of the crew, was a smoker, had the perpetual smoker's cough, and whenever he laughed at some joke or story, would be momentarily convulsed by paroxysms of hacking. I would pull up an apple box in Fred's cabin, and we would make small talk about the day or swap stories until the evening grayed and I wandered home.

Fred puzzled me—perhaps that's why I liked spending time with him. He seemed out of place as a ranch hand, appeared to have more potential in life than most of the help. His careful attention to grooming and cleanliness—his bunk was always neatly made, his cabin swept and tidy—said much for his character. But I was young and did not understand the power of bourbon, for Fred was a drunk, a Jim Beam groupie. For days he would be fine, but there would come a Saturday when Fred would tumble off the wagon. The binge would start in town and carry over to his cabin where Fred would drain a fifth of whiskey, maybe more, until he drank himself into oblivion. The frontier writer Charlie Russell observed about alcohol: "If you want to know a man, get him drunk and he'll tip his hand; I ain't saying booze is good for men, but it boils what's in him to the top." Fred was a quiet drunk; the more he drank, the quieter he became, until the alcohol completely anesthetized him. And for the next few days the world went on without Fred Walters. After these bouts with the bottle, Fred returned to the world of the sober in a delicate condition, sallow-faced, jaundiced, his hands too unsteady to light a cigarette. In Fred's case Russell was correct: drunk or sober, I never recall seeing Walters angry once in all the seasons he came to the ranch.

Fred wintered in the flophouses of Portland, where I'm sure without the routine of work, his drinking continued on a more consistent basis. As I said, Fred was a handsome fellow and most likely never lacked for female companionship in the bars of Portland, probably spent his time in the tavern with a faded flower at each elbow, helping him drink up his year's wages. One evening in his cabin as I perched on my apple box opposite Fred, he told me of an encounter with one of these saloon klootches. Mr. Walters and the lady had cozied up to a table in a bar and were no doubt matching each other drink for drink when Fred groped her under the table, and then followed up with an obscene quip about the size of his date's private parts. The floozie exclaimed, "Why, honey, that's not very nice. You came out of one, you know!" "Yes, I did," Fred laughed, "But that's the first one I've found that I could climb back into!" With that compliment the woman yanked off her shoe, and flailing at Fred with her footwear, clocked him a good one on the head with her shoe and chased him from the bar. So ended Fred's romantic evening–and his female companionship. I had to wait nearly two minutes for Fred to stop coughing.

One year when spring returned, Fred did not. I believed him dead: maybe drunk to death in the bars of Portland, his cirrhotic liver shot, or perhaps mugged in some Portland alley, beaten to death by some weapon more substantial than a shoe. But I heard a rumor to the contrary: Fred had met a woman, married her, became a family man, and turned his life around. I would like to believe that rumor.

A gentleman in a slouch hat–that was the sum of Walt Webb. Walt was a tall, rangy fellow of middle-age. In his youth Walt must have been a dashing young man, for he was a striking fellow even in middle-age. He had the fresh, blushing complexion of a young girl, which complimented a head of thick, wavy, white hair. Though Walt wore a broad brimmed felt hat, he was not the typical ranch hand: he rented a house in town, drove to and from work, and when he drank, moderation was his excess. Walt had little patience with slackers or the silly antics of the young crew. If you went about your work, and did so with little nonsense, Walt was always friendly and had a kind word for you. In short, Walt Webb was urbanity in coveralls.

The violin was Walt's passion. He collected, repaired, and played them. On chilly nights fall and winter we would visit the small house on Bridge Street, settle in for the evening with Walt and his fiddle. Though I liked the music, those old Appalachian blue-grass tunes, what I loved even more was watching the man play. Standing there in the center of that warm little room, as if he were a subject in a Thomas Hart Benton painting, Walt leaned into his fiddle, his big fingers falling, drifting, sliding up and down the neck of the instrument, coaxing note after note of "A Maiden's Prayer," (my favorite) from the strings, cherry wood bow rising, falling with Walt's arm, dancing, gliding dangerously close to that slouch hat.

A patch of resin frosted the fiddle's midriff. As the music drew the room in close, the ashes from Walt's cigarette drooped pendant like a gray blossom. If you did not know Walt well, you knew him better when his fiddle sang. The scene was enough to make your eyes leak with feeling.

Men like Walt were my early studies in character there on the ranch by the river. There were nameless others, like the cultured bum who despised the poetry of Goldsmith and delighted in the art of Jackson Pollack. And one whose name was Harry, a ruggedly handsome man, dashing enough to be a **GQ** model, but chose instead the hardworking, hard drinking life of a drifter, working for the man. Perhaps that is why I found myself in familiar territory when I read Steinbeck. I knew his people: Candy, Crooks, Slim, and George; they were my people, too. I had worked alongside them, sat in their bunkhouses, heard their stories, earned their friendship and trust. In my contact with them, I had brushed against the rough edges of life and enriched my own.

Messing About in Boats

> Believe me, my young friend, there is **nothing**—absolutely nothing—half so much worth doing as simply messing about in boats. Simply messing, messing—about—in—boats—messing—

> River Rat
> *The Wind in the Willows*

One summer when the river was in flood, two young men in a canoe paddled ashore below our house. They were voyaging, we learned, from the mouth of the Columbia to its Canadian headwaters. I was in awe of the two explorers and their gleaming canoe. To me the two sun-burnished adventurers were like the French voyageurs, those frontiersmen of river commerce; I could not have been more impressed had they worn dashing red sashes and tasseled stocking caps jauntily perched on their heads. For half an hour they shared their adventures on the river, their exploits portaging around the dams (as they would Chief Joseph ten miles upstream). We wished to be part of their adventure, so we gave them a loaf of bread and wished them *bon voyage*. They boarded their graceful craft, swung into the backwater current, saluted us with their paddles, and glided silently upstream. I watched them thread their way through the islands of willow, watched until all I could see was the rhythmic glint from the dip and swing of their paddles. The next several days I thought about our two visitors often, wondered where they were on the river. And I thought about the romance of being on the river myself, freed from the tedium of shore, in tune with the river's fluid grace, its caprices of current and eddy. I too yearned to be a boatman, mess about in boats.

Each spring, two weeks before fishing season, Dad would call Otto Sartz at his Alta Lake marina and reserve a boat from his flotilla of neatly painted yellow and green skiffs. I learned to row in one of these little rowboats, to pull both oars together in a single stroke, to steer and turn the little craft on a dime. And it was because I wanted to captain my own ship, employ my fledgling skills as an oarsman that I found the newspaper ad. Someone in town had a rowboat for sale, a steal I thought, at twenty-five dollars, and I persuaded Dad to investigate.

We found the house in town. The owner led us to a forlorn backyard where in a pile of weeds and dead leaves, mired in the ground lay a little ruin of a rowboat. And even though a section of the port gunwale was dry rotted and stove in, I thought the derelict had promise: twenty-five dollars–seemed a real bargain to me. Dad had his doubts, told the seller we would think it over and let him know later.

Dad, far more skilled at boat building and carpentry than I, and knowing the labor such a project would entail, wanted to turn his back on the whole deal. For my part, I had already taken possession of the relic. Then began the pleading, cajoling, begging, and in less than a week the little derelict had come aground in our backyard. It took Dad months to repair the rowboat. He did the job right, replaced the broken, decayed gunwale panel in the precise, fastidious manner Dad always brought to any project. Dad painted "our" little skiff a cheerful red and lettered the name *Folly* in white on her prow. I somehow felt the name was meant as an aspersion against me: my folly that Dad bought the boat; his folly that he conceded to my foolish whim. Which of the two inspired the name I never did learn. Suffice it to say the labor and love Dad invested in refitting the little boat was sufficient for him to assume its full ownership. Again, I was a captain without a ship, and so remained until a small stroke of providence sailed one my way, and although I couldn't claim ownership, I pretty much had the use of her anytime I wished.

Mr. Bill Gebhardt, the camp mechanic, brought his wooden rowboat to the ranch to assist in positioning the intake pipe of the home place pump and moored it next to the pump house beside the Owl Thicket. "Mr. Beehart" we called him because he kept bees was a thickset German. It was Gebhardt who fostered my interest in beekeeping, helped me establish my first colony, and became my beekeeping mentor. Bill had his own machine shop on a lot in town where he and his wife Marie lived in a tiny clapboard cabin. The Gebhardts purchased and cleared fifteen acres of rattlesnake infested sagebrush at the end of the county road across the river from Pateros and planted the acreage in apples. They kept their day jobs: Bill, the camp mechanic; Marie, a teller at the Brewster Bank, until their young orchard began to bear. In the meantime they spent every spare hour tending their new planting.

The Gebhardts were sturdy Old Country stock, used to farming and hard work. Marie was a rough and tumble character, personable, but the no nonsense type. If Marie had sparred a round or two with George Roenfranz, I would have bet even money on the outcome. According to my friend Dorothy Lewis, a good friend of Marie's, (the two were cast from the same mold) on hot summer days Marie would strip off her top and go about her work clothed in nothing but levis and a bra. Their new orchard was plagued by gophers, and Bill hired me to thin the population. Privy to Dorothy's information about Marie's summer attire, I walked my trapline warily, especially if the day was a scorcher, more afraid of encountering a sweating, half-naked Marie than a big sage rattler. From Marie I got an 1879 silver dollar from the bank; from Bill, my life-long affinity for bees. And the use of his rowboat.

Sunday morning. The heat of the day yet a hint and a promise. The river, an icy rush of swollen melt water, chill enough to burn a swimmer's breastbone, tinge it pink, set it afire, flows down the valley. Only the bold–and for seconds only–would dare duck his head in the blue-green cold. Again, it is Sunday, and my family sleeps, respite from the week's routine, gathering strength for Sunday school and church. Morning belongs to me, to me and the gray doves crouched in their crude nests, crooning across the still air. I slip from the house and make my way through the willows to the riverbank where the boat awaits. I loose the skiff from the mooring, shove off, jump aboard and unship the oars.

Bill's boat was plywood, flat keeled, wide beamed, and sorely in need of paint. The flaking shards insinuated a past of green. The grain of the right oar was weathered, split, and I pulled it with caution, ever watchful the fissure closed against the stroke. Though the craft was weathered and well-used, it was seaworthy enough, leaked very little.

That still morning I pulled away from shore and rowed in the calmer backwater, staying well clear of the river's main race else I be swept downstream a mile or so before I could reach shore. Owl Thicket was submerged in the flood. As I glided over the covert, the willowy withes swirled beneath the keel, swayed, spun and twisted to the music of the current, like the olive-green tresses of some sea hag weathering a tempest. Often an upsurge of water, a ricochet off an obstacle in the depths, would roil the surface, testify to the force of the river. Occasionally one of these current blooms would explode beneath the skiff. Then the boat would spin and whirl off course. I thought it curious that unless I caught one of these sudden explosions, I had little other sense of movement. Even when I pulled through a stroke, it was as if only my body moved. If I did not look at the shore, I seemed, for all my efforts to be at rest, idle, as if afloat in a lake. I rowed in and around the islands of willow, gliding as far upriver from breakfast as I dared, then came booming back home on the current to claim my share of scrambled eggs and bacon, that special Sunday morning fare.

During the high water season driftwood collected along the log booms behind the dam. Periodically, these booms would be cleared, releasing the assorted flotsam to cascade down spillways and drift downriver. It was great fun to row among sticks, chunks of bark, and logs. I saw the wood drifts as firewood, free for the taking, and rowed through the detritus, hauling aboard anything I could pull from the water. On one driftwood foray I piled my borrowed craft nearly to the gunwales before I headed to shore. Once, floating among one driftwood spill I found a pine saw log that had somehow escaped from a logging operation upriver. This behemoth was a thirty footer nearly three feet in diameter—the bark alone was inches thick. I was able to get a line on it, laid my back into the oars and with much effort towed the log ashore just upriver from the house.

For three or four seasons that big stick of Ponderosa rested on the bank. I set myself the task of chopping through the thing and whenever I felt the need for exercise or the desire to strike something, I took the big single bit ax, my inheritance from Grandpa Fike, and laid into the log. Though I raised many a blister swinging the heavy blade, my lumberjack moments had little effect on the log. I lost interest barely six inches into the project, and one spring I gave the lonesome pine its freedom, released it from the tether. One day I returned from school to find the leviathan gone, reclaimed by the flood. I had left my mark, though, a ragged notch, barely more than a blaze. A yearling beaver would have scoffed at the effort.

I dared not attempt a river crossing during high water. To brave the full race of current would have been foolhardy; I would have been swept miles downriver before I reached the opposite bank at Pateros seven miles downstream. In late summer and fall after the river purged itself of the spring flood, when the water receded to safe levels, I found I could cross at will by using the slower backwaters and eddies along the river bar upriver from the house. In the calmer waters I was able to row upriver to the head of the bar. Here the river narrowed and the current raced. Now I had my work cut out for me. I swung the boat into the teeth of the river and bent my back into the oars. In this manner I was able to move cross river on a diagonal heading. Still, at low water I lost half a mile or so before I reached the eddies on the opposite shore. The main current eased me into the sluggish backwaters which swung upriver. Rowing easily now, I could progress upstream as far as the small bay offshore Lynne Hymer's house. Once I beached the boat on the sandbar below her house and came ashore for a surprise visit. The homeward voyage I rowed leisurely cross current, reaching with ease the inlet by the home place pump where the boat was moored.

Only one time did I catch the school bus in Okanogan County, and only once did I get off at the same stop. I loved being on the river in the early morning, and one day an hour or so before time to catch the bus for school, I took the boat out for a cross river jaunt. I made the crossing and puttered about in the eddy offshore of the big boulder where in the fall Dad came often to fish. I let the eddy carry me upriver a bit. Then I'd swing the prow into the main current and drift downriver again. After two or three of these drifting cycles, I realized I had lost track of time. I would have to do some serious rowing to cross the river in time to catch my ride to school. I gave the oars a powerful sweep, but in my haste I forgot to position the right oar against the weathered crack. With a sharp snap the oar broke in two just below the oarlock. Grasping the now useless stump of oar, I watched helplessly as the paddle floated away down current.

Fortunately I was not far offshore when the oar snapped. Had I been trying the main current, I might have gone to school that day in Pateros, had to shift my allegiance to the Billygoats. Unlike a V-keeled canoe, the flat-bottomed craft did not respond well to the side paddle technique, wanted to slip sideways, turn in circles. And so with much frantic paddling, like a wounded duck, I was able to reach the bank several revolutions later and moor the rowboat.

My schoolmates the Millers lived a quarter mile up the bank from where I came ashore. (Mrs. Miller was my seventh grade substitute teacher.) I hurried uphill to their house, reached it in time to call Mom, inform her of my mishap, and then catch the school bus at Millers' stop. The next day I purchased a new oar at Dick Bennett's hardware store, and after school with school books under one arm and a gleaming new oar under the other, I boarded the Millers' bus for the return trip. And that afternoon with a sturdy, new oar in the oarlock, I ferried myself home from school.

Bill Gebhardt quit the ranch to tend his orchard full time. His rowboat went with him, thus concluding my rowing days on the river. But I was a powerboat enthusiast by then, in particular an avid hydroplane fan. Ray Glessner, our pastor and my Sunday school teacher, built a small hydroplane, an eight footer of the "punkin seed" design, and in this little speedster scooted up and down the river to his favorite steelhead haunts. I marveled at Ray's bravado; in his tiny "buzzy horn" (young Barclay Crane's onomatopoeia for the screaming engines that powered these little craft around the race course) he ventured downriver around the bend below Pateros and beyond. In evenings he would return, skimming by the house, the nether stretches of the river and a day's fishing behind him.

One Sunday after the lesson, I asked Ray if he would build me a boat like his little two-seater. Ray agreed. Seventy-five dollars for materials and labor and I would be the owner of a slick little speedster myself. My vision for my little plywood shingle sprung from a color photo of Hawaii Kai III, one of my favorite hydroplanes. In the photo the powerboat skimmed supreme, lady-like, in pink glory across a sapphire surface. I would paint my little lady an exotic pink after the fashion of the Kai. Thus in her big sister's image I brushed my boat stem to stern a passionate pink.

On a wooden stanchion in the sporting goods section of Dick Bennett's hardware store sat a row of outboard engines. One stood out from the rest, a six horsepower Mercury outboard. To me it was the most beautiful piece of machinery I had ever seen. I never left the store without taking an admiring turn or two around this little jewel. With its delicate turquoise cowling and gleaming white gear housing to me it seemed a gem; I lusted in its presence. What better color to compliment my pastel little lady, colors meant for each other, a study in pink and turquoise, just the powerplant I needed to whisk my little craft and me across the water.

The little six horse engine had push button drive. I knelt on the turquoise boat cushions, my excitement bordering on fear. The engine idled softly. Beneath the stern, exhaust bubbles murmured, bubbled through the clear water of Alta Lake. My family watched from the boat launch. Push that black button, begin my maiden voyage. The little pink shingle drifted downwind toward a thicket of reeds, engine idling in neutral, yet I could not push that black button, throw the engine in gear. I was in the moment but could not make it happen. If Dad had not nodded agreement, I might have disappeared into the reed patch, his son the fool. I reached back, hit the button, felt the propeller catch, the little boat tremble. Turning my back on the shore, and right hand on the throttle, I steered the prow toward open water.

I twisted the throttle hard and the six horses stood the boat nearly on end like a pink finger. I shifted my weight forward, the bow dropped, and I shot off on plane, out of breath either from wind rush or excitement. Wave slap thrilled my knees. Over my shoulder, over the turquoise throb of the Mercury, the boat launch receded to a cleft in the shore. The keel split the lake, a wake of foam and wave curled aside the blue. And in that backward glance we became a photograph, a pink image skimming blue waters, casting them aside: my little hydro, me, in our pink splendor were the Kai.

Though I was a couple thousand horsepower shy of the big boats, I customized my little racer for maximum illusion of power and speed. I fastened two metal scoops either side of the motor mount flush with the keel. These devices created miniature roostertails, the hallmark of speed in the boat racing community, and were adjustable for effect. Though the gadgets did send spray skyward, I soon removed them because the effect looked contrived and the drag was noticeable.

The little Glessnercraft gave me many hours of enjoyment on the lake, and with it the two of us explored the far side of Alta accessible only by water. I now had the means to fish out of the way locations seldom fished, though I do not believe any of these yielded a catch superior to the customary fishing holes. Our friends, the Gibbs, let me store the boat and motor at their lake cabin, a convenience that precluded us having to haul the combination to and from the ranch in the station wagon. For some reason I never ran the boat on the river. Only once did I operate it in waters other than Alta and then to ill effect. To this day I can't imagine what lunacy led me to believe I could navigate my tiny craft the entire length of the Okanogan River from confluence to its headwaters at Oroville where it spilled from Lake Osoyoos. And though wisdom is seldom an attribute of the young, I must have been totally bereft. (Even Ray Glessner would have dismissed the idea as sheer lunacy, I'm sure.)

I have mentioned earlier our summer vacations to Oroville and Lake Osoyoos. Now that I had a powerboat of my own, I thought of the fun I could have cruising the waters of Osoyoos. There was the matter, however, of transporting the boat the ninety miles to Oroville. The station wagon had no luggage rack, nor did I own a trailer. Because the car would be packed to the tailgate with camping gear, the usual transport with the back seat and tailgate down was no option. Surely Dad must have had misgivings about my bold adventure, but if he did, I don't recall, and being a teenager and headstrong, I'm sure I scoffed at any fears as unwarranted.

(Perhaps Dad's own youthful adventures on the high seas tempered his judgment, turned him from adversary to advocate. Sailing a small homemade canvas boat across Elliott Bay, Dad and his twin brother Mike were caught in a sudden storm. A passing freighter spotted the tempest-tossed little craft, its young crew, and sped to their aid. Dad and Mike, who were enjoying their romp through the heavy seas, and not the least bit frightened, waved the steamer off.

The crew, their rescue attempt thwarted, did the next best thing: they sailed alongside the bobbing coracle and tossed the boys fresh oranges and other treats before continuing their passage.)

We put in downriver from the Monse bridge, hauled the outboard and two tanks of gas (our estimate for the four hour trip to Oroville) down the bank, and said our good-byes. I settled my knees into the boat cushions, started the engine, popped the button into gear. I drifted to midstream and set out.

My odyssey lasted scarcely three minutes. Barely had I reached full plane and top speed when the engine screamed. For some reason the engine had tilted up; the prop was throwing water everywhere. For a moment I was confused, panicked, but had sense enough to kill the engine. Then I realized what had happened: though I was midstream, I had run full tilt upon a gravel bar, aground for sure. I looked over the side where the current rushed over the mottled gravel barely one foot below the surface.

Dad had stopped upriver on the Monse bridge to watch me skim along beneath, wave *bon voyage*. When I failed to show, he retraced the river downstream. He found what must have been a pitiful sight. Amid tears and gravel, ankle deep in the current, there I stood, naked except for a swim suit, clinging desperately to the bow cleat. I was never so glad to see my dad. That aborted voyage on the Okanogan was the first and only time I tried river navigation in the little pink lady. (I sold my first love to Mervyn Gragg, who did pilot her on the big river, powered to and fro by a little Elgin outboard, which had hitherto run only in the oily waters of a fifty gallon drum in Mervyn's backyard.)

I briefly powerboated the Columbia myself. Hans Moen owned a marina in Bridgeport and raced outboard hydros. I bought one from him, stripped the varnish from the mahogany, painted the racer a dark blue, and emblazoned the prow with a showy flame job. Hans tuned the thirty horsepower Mercury racing engine, even selected a competitive propeller, but I never participated in a single race. And though that Mercury engine could push the little craft to nearly sixty miles an hour, the only danger I ever encountered came from shore. One day as I planed the stretch of river opposite camp and the cold storage shed, showing off, I admit, I heard a loud thud and looked up just in time to see a stone the size of a hen's egg carom off the bow. On the bank by the cold storage I saw a large figure doubled over in laughter, pointing a long arm in my direction. Ivan Kimball, one of the crew and a giant of a man, had pegged a rock nearly a hundred and fifty yards and plunked the hydro. When I angrily confronted him later, he was still laughing. "You could have killed me!" I spluttered. Ivan's response: "I sure got your attention, didn't I! Your head popped up like a turkey in a corn patch!" I used nearly a half cup of filler to patch the dent, then sold the boat, flames and all, back to Hans. Messing about in boats provided too much variety for me—especially with an arm like Ivan's lurking bankside.

Dogs and Cats and Animals...

Those who choose to share their lives with dogs will tell you that each canine companion demarks a portion of their own lives. One day the neighbor's dog, a tousled dust mop of an animal, came up missing. The neighbor combed the roadside several yards from the house and found the dog lying on the shoulder, a victim, as veterinarians call it, of rubber poison. My neighbor, a burley, bow-legged man who had spent a good many years around horses, training them, riding them, being battered and busted up by them, told me he stood by the side of the road and wept unashamedly over the pet that had seen him through two divorces and one bankruptcy. His tears, I believe, were manifestations, not so much of grief over the loss of a pet, but the metaphorical expression of those years of his own life irrevocably linked to his companionship with the deceased.

PUPPY LOVE

With Tiny, it was puppy love, love at first sight, my singular infatuation with a blonde (Penny Matthieson excepted, though in that relationship I was bewitched by the charm of looks). Tiny and I grew up together. In those years I screamed at him; I humiliated him; and once in anger I even shot at him (just in his general direction, my shot deflected by exasperation). To these various outrages Tiny always returned a love unswerving and unconditional.

Tiny's mother belonged to Ralph Dobson. When I heard she was to have a litter, I asked Ralph to reserve me a pup. He agreed. I had a sentimental interest in the litter: the sire of this batch belonged to my friend Mickey Schultz—and I was a close friend to both. Like most of the ranch mongrels, Mickey's dog had a curious bloodline, a colorful blend of canine ethnicity that in his case was strong on spaniel with the underpinning of some longer legged breed. The result was a dog whose locomotion appeared to be on stilts, as if he had been forewarned of an imminent flood. His tail was docked, his coat a snarl of blonde cow licks. The dog had a penchant for ripe fruit, pears in particular, which he would snatch from a low hanging branch. As if propelled by a spring, he would bound into the foliage, emerge with a fat D'Anjou clenched in his jaw, then retreat somewhere to shade and gnaw his prey to the core. Mick's dog was a constant companion on our hunting trips and jaunts afield. (Once, he blundered into a patch of prickly pear. Whining plaintively amid the thorny patch, the dog refused to budge until we extracted him from the prickers, his paws festooned with cactus spines like pin cushions. We took turns carrying him home.) When reprimanded, he became hangdog and according to Mick, "looked over his glasses" at you until forgiven. Mick named his dog Tiny, I guess, because that seemed an apt name for a puppy. I named my own pup after his father. Tiny came to me in a newspaper-lined cardboard box. He was mine for fourteen years.

I am lying on my back in the clothesline yard. A knot of blonde fury worries my hair. I sling my head and fling the fury off. Growling in puppy rage, Tiny pounces on my face, dives into my hair, fetches a mouthful in his milk teeth. I can smell his pablum breath as he digs in and pits three pounds of puppy wrath against my hair. I sit up, flip him on his back. Above, Tiny's soft fur is tow head blonde, awash with curls; below, belly swollen, mottled like a pinto bean. I cup my hand just above his brush-tipped node of a penis, clasp his belly and roll him left and right. Little needle teeth clamp down on my thumb and forefinger. Growls and snarls feign combat. I release him and lie back. Again he is in my face. This time the musky pablum smell washes over me as the pup laps my eyes, cheeks, and nose, my mouth with a frenzied tongue. I snatch him up, hold him aloft, his grunts and growls thrill through my hands, my arms—my heart. He squirms to be released. This way we spend hours during his puppyhood. Bonding. I doubt he could love me as much as I love him. Puppy love.

Though ordinary enough as a pup, in his transition to adult Tiny underwent a curious metamorphosis. He looked nothing whatsoever like his sire and namesake. His mongrel heritage caused a curious somatype. The thistledown blonde seasoned to rich cinnamon; he came up short–literally–of his father's height and weight. (Even well-fed he tipped the scales at less than twenty-five pounds, I'm sure.) Fore, he was thick maned, leonine; aft, lean, tapering off to an expressive tail (unlike his father's docked stub), set in motion by any friendly word. Somewhere, Tiny's family tree forked into Chow: his tongue was black. He had the ears and muzzle of a spaniel, and chestnut eyes, benevolent, prescient, like a Madonna's. And the heart of a lion. The rest was all mutt. His hybrid vigor kept the doctor away; never once in his fourteen years did he see a veterinarian.

Tiny was prone to fits of excitement. These we would encourage (incite?) with a chant-like cry at which he would disappear at breakneck speed around the house. As soon as he reappeared, in chorus we would resume our cries and send him dashing off for another circuit. Three of these were usually his limit. Then he would sit nearby, panting, black tongue lolling in, out, nearly to the grass, grinning in joy as if to say, "What fun that was!" Any attention shown him, Tiny would return many-fold.

When he ran full out, Tiny could fairly fly, but when there was no need for hurry, he ran with a curious lope. His hindquarters would track right awhile, then switch left. It was a sideways shift, hind feet kicking up dust to his right for a few feet, then the rhythm would shift left, like one of those cars whose frame has been sprung, as if the rear end wanted to swap ends with the front. And thus he would lope to greet you, always grinning that "glad to see you" grin.

Something's Rotten in the Neighborhood

Tiny had a proclivity for strong smells, especially if they came in the shape of a skunk. He would go out of his way to investigate any black and white intruder on the place: in short, Tiny was a skunk's welcome wagon. Spring nights when the skunks were particularly active, a heavy musk always hung in the air. Sometimes the odor signified a black and white in the neighborhood. Mostly, however, the stench came from Tiny—and we would know what he had been up to sometime during the night. Then it would be necessary to distance ourselves from the dog for two or three days until the smell subsided.

From a safe distance I watched many an encounter between dog and skunk, and they always played out in the same way. Tiny would waylay the interloper, who nonchalantly sized up his adversary. The meeting would begin face to face, then quickly turn to in your face—Tiny's. I always knew when the skunk scored a direct hit. There would be a break in the action while Tiny rolled in the dust, snorted and sneezed in attempt to clear his sinuses of the putrid spray. After the respite he would return to the quarry and resume the fray. This scenario would continue until I called off my dog.

Once out of sadistic curiosity I wanted to see just what my little companion was made of, discover his olfactory threshold of skunk juice, his staying power. Tiny and I were passing the home place pump when he did a double take at a pile of twelve inch pipe used to extend the pipeline when the river dropped. Immediately Tiny began his critter bark, a blend of impassioned whine and yelp, at the mouth of the pipe. "Go get, 'em, Tiny!" and the fun began. Tiny darted into the pipe and amidst metallic echoes of yips and yelps, bailed out in reverse and headed for the deepest dust in the middle of the road. Nine "Go get 'em's" later Tiny was still on the offensive. I called off my dog only after the skunk, which had given ground to the end of the pipe, left its cover, and perplexed by Tiny's tenacity, turned teeth to the enemy, tried to bite him. (I had heard skunks carried rabies and Tiny had never seen a vet.). Just what it was in his nature that made him a scourge of skunks I never understood. (Some of the camp dogs, foolish in other ways, fell afoul of porcupines. Tiny never did. He bayed one once and kept a healthy distance between his tender nose and the critter's flailing tail. Only once did I remove quills from Tiny: they were in his back. He had rolled in a dead porcupine, the fragrance of which may have been skunk-like.) But come the end of spring, all the fur would be burned from the ridge of his nose.

Summers, for variety, Tiny would switch fragrances, come up from the river bank slicked down with pomade of dead squawfish, grinning like a kid on his first date, only to slink away amid exhortations of reproof and disgust. And for three more days we would be strangers again.

A' Hunting We Will Go

On the occasion of his dog's demise, the sportsman and writer Franklin Burroughs eulogized his hunting companion's life with the summation: "His life's work came to forty-six grouse." No desecration intended but Burroughs' dog was a slacker compared to Tiny. Tiny was a hunting fool; he brought to the field the same passion and dedication to the hunt as he did to harassing skunks. Step out the door with a shotgun, rifle—any object resembling a barrel—and the result would be instant canine ecstasy. Up the road we would go—no command necessary—I, cradling a shotgun, Tiny, leaping, bounding, turning back flips around me like a drum major in a two man parade. (While I was away at college, Peter Crane told me that every time he walked by the house with a firearm, the result was the same: he had an immediate hunting companion as long as he was afield.)

Anyone who has hunted upland game birds without a dog has experienced the surprise burst of pheasant, grouse or covey of quail from an adjacent covert of sagebrush and stood there in confusion, unable to get off a shot, shotgun at half mast, while the birds sailed off unscathed. For game birds, you need a buffer to temper that element of surprise. You need a hunting dog, and I set out to train Tiny for the hunt. I gleaned training tips from *Sports Afield*, *Outdoor Life*, and other sporting magazines. Somewhere I read that a cardinal rule of training a hunting dog was to discourage the student from hunting or killing vermin or any other non-game animal. (I didn't know it then, but Tiny would hunt anything: if there was game in the neighborhood, he would find it, roust it out, be it a solitary quail, rabbit or deer.) Such behavior was sure to be habit forming: your dog would go the way of the proverbial egg sucking dog: suck one egg, and he was a sucker for life. Therefore, when Tiny's first kill was a mouse, I was horrified: did I want a hunter whose focus was rodents? My dog, a cat? I confiscated the mouse, slipped a string noose around its head, and looped the whole affair around Tiny's neck, all the while spewing a diatribe of reproach and rebuke at the unfortunate dog. For two days Tiny wore his mouse pendant of shame.

Keeping my hunting companion reined in proved to be a particular challenge. Once in the field, Tiny's enthusiasm often carried him beyond shotgun range: birds would take flight far ahead, at too great a distance for me to down them. No amount of shouting deterred him then. Time and again the birds would flush yards ahead, well beyond even the range of a twelve gauge. Sometimes the whirring of wings or the chortle of a sped ringneck would be my only connection with the game. Then when the game was fled, Tiny would slink back sheepishly. I would vent my anger, shower him with every imaginable curse. In frustration I nearly gave up on him, determined to go it alone, but when I commanded him to stay, it was as if something died in him. In disbelief he would begin to follow but a "Stay!" sharper than the first froze him in his tracks. Then he looked so downright miserable I would recant, and some time later in the hills Tiny would bound off again, scattering any game in the vicinity to kingdom come, oblivious to the curses flung his way. And with Tiny slinking behind, I would trudge home in silence, pretending he didn't exist.

Leash training Tiny to heel, which kept him in close until I was ready to work, helped some. But the first two years we hunted together, Tiny's urge to romp off ahead continued to be a problem. Gradually we became a team. Tiny learned to associate the gunshot with downed game (this was Tiny's payoff: to be up close and personal with what he knew by scent only): no shot, no carcass. And so he learned to work closer in. I learned, too, learned to read his movements in the field, which zig meant birds, which zag cottontails, for Tiny compensated for the game of the moment. At the command, "Go get, 'em, Tiny!" he would dart from my side and begin casting through the sagebrush. Tiny's movements were plot and narrative of the hunt, like a honeybee's waggle dance on the comb. Casting from side to side, for instance, signified a covey of birds, as Tiny would spring from one scent to the next, following the birds' zigzag feeding pattern. Longer runs meant a solitary bird, say a pheasant or a sharptail grouse. Run full out in a straight line and Tiny had a rabbit in his nose hairs.

I loved to watch him run a rabbit, especially from a vista where I could watch the entire drama unfold below. On one such encounter Tiny was so intent on the quarry he failed to see a badger hole, hit the depression flat out, went airborne, and like the coyote in the cartoon somersaulted a full gainer and a half. He hit the ground in full stride and a cloud of dust and continued his beeline as if he had planned the maneuver. Most of Tiny's rabbit encounters were by scent only; rarely did he catch sight of the cottontail. I always knew when he did. Then Tiny would issue a yelp solely reserved for rabbits. It was a singular yip: I can only describe it as a blended cry of pain and glee. When Tiny ran a rabbit, I always knew where to look for the game—first, find Tiny, then look 180 degrees the opposite direction. Almost always you would see the rabbit somewhere along the backtrack, loping along, putting distance and safety between his cottontail and the frenzied dog. Most of the time Brer Rabbit would not even bother to den up.

Whenever I got off a shot, Tiny would bound high two or three times in the direction of the shot, trying to locate the falling bird or tumbled rabbit, his ears hoisted full staff to hear the game connect with the ground. I always had a good laugh at these antics and sometimes, distracted by my own dog, had trouble locating the game myself.

I had little skill as a dog trainer—and more to the truth, even less patience—so I never taught Tiny to point or retrieve. But together we developed our own style, and seldom did we return from a hunt empty handed. On one safari in Chapman's peach orchard I knocked down a pheasant. The bird tried to rise again but failed, and I knew then it would be a footrace between Mr. Ringneck and Tiny. I followed them at a trot, kept Tiny in sight for half a mile when he disappeared into Kirk's pear orchard. I caught up to Tiny deep in the orchard, found my dog mid-row, panting away, that triumphant grin on his face, the winded pheasant pinned gently beneath his paws. We bagged another that day, and at home I snapped a photo of a smiling Tiny silhouetted against the back wall of the house, proudly posed beside the brace of birds, each nearly his size.

No, I did not teach Tiny to retrieve, but to my surprise, retrieve he could—and did. On that occasion we were dove hunting on the river bar upriver of the Owl Thicket. The doves, after gorging themselves in the wheat fields above, came whistling down the hills seeking water and grit at the river bar. At dusk, heavily laden like bombers on a bomb run, they would clamber aloft, head for their roosts. I tumbled one in a storm of feathers and watched in dismay as it splashed down in the river a few yards off shore. The current caught the pile of feathers and swung it downriver. I was not one to waste game and in desperation I gave the command, "Go get, 'em, Tiny!" Tiny, who had been crowhopping along the bank in excitement, needed no more encouragement. To my surprise he leaped into the water, swam to the dove, and labored back to the bank with the bird fast in his jaws. Tiny climbed ashore and deposited the wet mass of feathers at my feet. I picked up the limp pile. A pendulum of entrails dangled from its posterior. The body was spatchcocked; I doubt there was a single bone unbroken. Tiny had what the bird dog circles termed a "hard mouth." But no matter—I was ecstatic: I had myself some hunting dog. In our hunting days together Tiny retrieved perhaps a half dozen doves from the river. In spite of commands to take it easy, be gentle, each bird reached shore as the first, gutted and crushed.

I left the house on the river, off to college, and Tiny stayed behind to watch over the family, guard them against skunks. He was their dog then, always on call should one need a hiking companion or wish to go hunting. But when I returned for holidays or summers, Tiny was mine again, once more my companion and partner afield. I had bought a '48 Ford pickup, and Tiny rode shotgun on our trips to Paradise Hill for grouse or snowshoe rabbits or to the bluffs above Bonita Flats for chukar, or the occasional fishing overnighter up the Methow where he kept me awake all night growling at the dark. Just the words "Go for a ride?" and Tiny hopped into the cab, sat smiling, anxious to be on the road, ready for whatever adventures lay ahead.

When I married and left the riverbank for good, Tiny was already old. I do not know much about his life those days, if he spent his time at ease, lying in the sun, if the family, with their busy lives and routines paid him much attention, or if he still made the occasional trip to Cranes' to steal the food–and dish–of Cranes' German Shepherd Marten. (Once Tiny and Marten passed each other in the driveway, each carrying the other's dog dish firmly in his teeth.) In those days I would like to think Tiny missed me, wondered where I was, when we would be together again in the hills. That is what I want to believe.

> Tiny rests in his old bedspread by the flagpole. Neither does he live on the riverbank these days. Though the family he loves lives here, this is not his home. I sit beside him, say his name, and he moves to my voice as did the old hound Argos to Odysseus's upon his master's return to Ithaca. With effort he lifts his head, sniffs recognition, softly thumps his tail, then settles again into the old bedspread and is still. We sit together. In memory our adventures call, this dog of mine, this friend who knows all my secrets. It is our last moment together.

> Some days later Mom's letter arrives: "...Tiny was 'gone' Monday morning...so faithful and friendly–not a mean streak in him...Dad and Kevin buried him on the

hill across from the house...made a little cross...left him
wrapped in the bedspread...."

I have a photo of Tiny—no doubt one of his last. In
it, eyes dimmed, presenting a tired smile to the camera,
sits an old dog. His shadow stretches dark across the lawn.
For such a little dog he cast a long shadow. Across our
lives. Across our hearts.

Stand by Your Dog

Let this serve as a post script, for it involves Tiny, though
I am its main concern, a boy in error and the man who showed that
boy a kindness. In those days Tiny shared the ranch with numerous other dogs. There was eccentric Marten, Cranes' bumbling
German Shepherd who would spend hours on the river bank with a
river cobble for a playmate. In spite of their difference in size, Tiny
and Marten got along well. Tiny also tolerated Dusty and Goldie,
Dale Piggot's two frenetic golden shepherds, whose guardianship
I undertook when Dale was diagnosed with tuberculosis and sent
packing to a sanitarium for treatment. The Lowrance's dachshund
Tina (to irritate the Lowrance boys Mike and Wayland we called
her Teener the Weener) occasionally swung by and helped herself
to Tiny's food, which he shared with no apparent misgivings. The
other camp dogs, a half dozen of which ran together in a pack, had
issues with Tiny and bullied him unmercifully. Perhaps his size made
the pack think he was easy pickings, but Tiny was a scrapper; never
once did I see him back down from a foe.

(Case in point: In camp there was a mother cat so protective
of her kittens she would not let a dog within a dozen feet of them.
Violate that space and the hapless mutt would soon be ki-yi-yipping
up the road in cloud of dust, wearing a berserk mama cat for a hair-
piece. One day mama, her kittens in tow, was crossing Cranes' lawn
en route to a mousing lesson. I decided to test Tiny's mettle, pit
my dog against the camp vixen, and sicced him on mama. Instantly,
in comic strip fashion, the scene exploded in whirling orbits of
fur. The affair lasted only seconds. Tiny emerged smiling from the

melee, mama cat glaring down at him from her perch on high in an old common delicious tree, each of the six kittens clinging to a prop, waiting for further instructions. No doubt about it—Tiny was a duelist of the very first house.)

I doubt any single dog would have gone one-on-one with Tiny, but the pack hated the very sight of him. A dogfight is a vicious spectacle, a primal scene that rends your ears like bone through a meat grinder. And I saw several with Tiny as principal. Once when he and I rode the crew truck home for lunch, we passed the roaming pack. There was an exchange of snarls. To avenge the affront, Tiny leaped from the bed of the speeding truck, hit the ground in a ball, and rolled into the midst of flying bodies and slashing teeth. I could not help him, was sure he would be torn to shreds. Though Tiny survived this attack and many others, he would emerge shaken, fur matted with slobber, sometimes bloodied.

The leader of the pack belonged to Bud Shenyer, the camp mechanic. A black dog of medium size—and like the other camp dogs, a mongrel—Blackie—we called him, was personable enough with humans, but to his kind a bully and to Tiny a swarthy nemesis. (I believe the two were near cousins, the enmity thus internecine.) Whenever Tiny and I wandered into their space, Blackie would incite four or five of his cronies against him. The encounters with these hooligans became more frequent, increasingly vicious, so severe I feared for his life. Tiny, I decided, needed a body guard.

In the fall, as I mentioned, our house was plagued by rats. To deal with the intruders, I had customized some shot shells by replacing the lead pellets with kernels of barley and rock salt. Whenever Tiny and I went out together, I took to carrying my .410 and two or three of these special loads. I hoped the sting from the non-lethal pellets would encourage the incensed pack to disperse. Blackie and his gang wasted no time giving me the opportunity to test the strategy, and the next time the pack attacked, I fired a load of rock salt into the fray. The round had little effect; the fighting continued as fiercely as before. I fired a second round. This, too, proved ineffective. After much kicking and shouting, I was able to rescue Tiny.

I was angry, afraid for my dog. My next shot shells would pack more punch, and that evening I prepared two more. This time I left a half dozen lead pellets among the grains of rock salt. It was a foolish decision, a reckless thing to do. And to this day I regret the choice.

It pains me to conclude this story, for it has a violent and shameful end. And I relate it only because I need to tell how the compassion and empathy of a man tempered the rash act of a sixteen year old youth. Some days later Tiny and I were walking the county road between the 80 and the homeplace when we again encountered Blackie and his gang. They fell upon Tiny in the middle of the road. The fight removed to the shoulder, spilled down the bank and into the sagebrush. I rushed to the edge of the road. Somewhere below, under that roiling mass of fur, claws, and fangs, fighting for his life was Tiny. In anger I shouldered the shotgun, held my fire until a black blur surfaced from the snapping pile. I aimed and pulled the trigger. Amid the echo of the report I heard a yelp of pain. Blackie detached himself from the knot of dogs. Blood streamed from his face and down his jaw. One of the lead pellets had struck him in the left eye. My anger instantly drained to horror. After losing the support of their leader, the pack unraveled and fled, Blackie bringing up the rear in pain and confusion. I stood in shock by the side of the road holding the awful shotgun. Beside me Tiny panted in safety. I had done the most heinous thing I had ever done in my life: I had shot another man's dog, Bud Shenyer's. In anger I had shot his children's pet.

Whether I told Mom and Dad what I had done, and they told me to make it right; whether I took the initiative to do so on my own, I do not recall. None of this matters anyway. Bud Shenyer is what matters. In all of this Bud could have reacted in a number of ways: perhaps shot my dog to avenge the death of his. Another man might have. He could have called the law as others surely would have. He might have sought a lawyer, sued Dad, as might other men in today's litigious world. Bud did none of these. What he did do was talk man-to-man with kindness and understanding to the boy who shot his dog.

Bud and I decided Blackie's fate. The dog was suffering, would never be whole again. I would have to put him to death. And that noon hour carrying the .22 special, I met Bud at his pickup. We drove to his house where we found Blackie. Except for the swollen slit that was once his left eye, he seemed unharmed, and on command even leaped into the bed of the truck. Sitting next to him against the cab, the .22 cradled between my knees, Blackie and I began his final journey.

If not for the mystery of canine charity, I might have proved a man in all this. The enormity of what I had done, was about to do, struck me then, and I must have moaned in dismay—or whimpered—me, not the doomed dog nestled at my side. Blackie sensed my distress and at my cry ducked his head and licked my hand, the condemned consoling the executioner. When Bud stopped the pickup just off the road below the old Pasley place, my face was awash with tears.

We led Blackie down the bank and tied him to a bush. I stepped back half a dozen paces and pumped a cartridge into the chamber. Blackie sat patiently in the sun. I raised the rifle and aimed. Suddenly the barrel blurred: Blackie, the canyon—everything swam. I could not pull the trigger. I could shoot at a man's dog, but I could not look the animal in its remaining good eye, aim and pull the trigger. Overwhelmed by the finality of death, I was racked by sobs and stood clutching the rifle. One paroxysm after another swept over me. Bud waited until it was time, gently slipped the rifle from my grasp, and stepped forward. I covered my face and turned away. I remember nothing more: the shot, the deceased, the two of us returning to the truck, the trip back to the ranch, none of it. I believe as we walked up the bank Bud slipped his arm around my shoulders. It seems to me he did.

In the affair with Blackie I proved the craven throughout. Though I had caused it, I could not look at the dog in death. Nor was I man enough to extend Blackie the courtesy of a burial, the dignity of a grave, just left his hapless body to rot on the bank of a canyon. I regret this affront to decency; it shames me to this day.

Bud Shenyer died in 1987. I never made the effort to thank him for his charity, for the man he was at that moment, the moment when the boy failed. I regret this the most.

And Cats

On the ranch by the river I remember a continuous ebb and flow of cats. In spring feline fecundity swelled their numbers. The vernal nights were filled with fur and rent by caterwauling as randy males, impatient for their turn, jockeyed for the camp's feline ladies of the night. In the spring cat promiscuity ran amok, and come summer there was always a bounty of cats. Their numbers dwindled after harvest when the rodenticide *Endrin* was applied to the fields to reduce mice populations and prevent the rodents from girdling the trees during winter. Oddly enough, ranch natural selection carried off the strongest mousers: one meal of an *Endrin*-laced mouse and a cat's entire inventory of lives was bankrupt. You would find their stiff carcasses in irrigation ditches or on the riverbank, a line of blood from ruptured intestines dried black beneath their tails. Thus with the seasons burgeoned and ebbed this tide of cats.

There were the bunkhouse cats, befriended and cared for by the crew. These wandered in and out of cabins, lived beneath them, and in the case of the previously mentioned mother cat, littered there. A substantial band of cats based their operations from Cranes' back porch, garage, and rooftop.

There is something about a cat that brings out the mischief in a boy. The child in Wales, Dylan Thomas, delighted in snowballing the neighborhood cats. On warm summer nights armed with a homemade blowgun fashioned from three lengths of brass tubing, I would sneak off to Cranes to spitball their cats, carrying with me a pocketful of aluminum foil spitwads pressed and rolled to the caliber of my blowgun. Lurking beneath the eaves of the big ranch house like some rainforest pigmy armed with curare darts, I stalked the cats. Sometimes I found them on the porch; sometimes hunkered in a roof valley; sometimes perched in a tree or shrub. Then I would take aim and with a blast of air send an aluminum pellet flying in their direction. I had a range of some fifty feet, and though I seldom scored a direct hit, to my delight the clatter of a pellet striking close at hand sent my target scurrying in panic. I discovered if I fired a large wooden match, it would ignite on impact with the roof shingles. In the burst of flame two glowing orbs betrayed a startled cat before it broke for the roof peak and fled into the night. For at least one summer anyway I was the bane of cats. It is a wonder Cranes' house survived my incendiary assault.

The poet T.S. Eliot maintained a cat should have three names. In the case of the ranch cats, this feline etiquette was largely ignored: I only knew two bunkhouse cats to have names. Dennis Gragg had a big yellow tabby named Lucky. Lucky was one of the few cats I have known to respond to the sound of his name. To summon his cat Dennis would shout, "Heeeere Lucky Lucky, my keekawsun—aaah aaah!" and in seconds Lucky would come boiling from someplace in the orchard and begin threading his flanks in and around Dennis's ankles, purring like a chainsaw. And then there was Puddy One-Eye.

Puddy One-Eye was a black cat, the mascot of the riverbank bunkhouse above the island. Gaunt in his frayed pelt of jet, Puddy saw the world through one baleful, golden eye. The other winked out years before, a victim, no doubt, of a claw or fang: some dog perhaps caught Puddy short of a tree's safety, or some jealous tom defending his turf or queen. Thus the moniker Puddy One-Eye.

By the time I knew Puddy, I'm sure he had exhausted nearly his entire quota of lives. A sinister cat, his one gold eye-ball fixed you like a spell. But for his ocular handicap he might have been a witch's familiar, could have doubled for the cat Piewhacket in *Bell, Book, and Candle*. Whether out of pity or admiration, it was not hard to be fond of the old reprobate. Whatever else, the cat was a survivor. For that reason I did not mind keeping company with Puddy One-Eye–that is until the following incident severely strained our friendship.

The pride of my tackle box was a certain fly hook. Among the other artificial flies it shone like a jewel. The lure was a study in yellow, wings fashioned from the fletching of tiny citron birds, shank swaddled in saffron yarn and wrapped with a fine gilt thread. Above the barb jutted a tail of jaunty yellow bristles. I paid top price, a dollar, maybe for this little prize. It was suitable for framing.

One day I decided to put this little beauty to the test, grabbed up my tackle box and pole, and headed for the island. The trail to the riverbank passed Puddy One-Eye's bunkhouse, and as I wandered by Puddy himself left whatever business he had going in the snakeweed thickets to follow me to the river. We crossed the neck of the island to its head where the river ran deep and swift. I set the tackle box on a rock, snapped it open, and found the cheery fly among it drab cousins. I removed the lure and knotted it to my leader.

The purpose of an artificial fly is to defraud a fish, delude him with the promise of a meal; the allure of the fly must exist for the fish, not the fisher. Nowhere on this earth exists–or existed–any insect or species of ephemera that bore the slightest resemblance to my lure. A half hour of casts and not so much as a minnow's nibble, confirmed my suspicions: the gilded fly was a masterpiece and apparently in the world of fish, as in our own, touching a work of art was taboo. I retrieved my fly, returned to the tackle box for a jar of salmon eggs. If nothing else the extra weight would gain me a few feet on my casts.

From the jar, I selected a plump egg and threaded it along the shank of the hook beneath the yellow bristles, careful not to expose the barb. I set the baited fly on a rock and returned the bait jar to the box. I had laid my pole against a boulder while I upped my ante with the fish egg. Now I retrieved it, lifted the rod, and looked behind me where I expected to see the egg laden fly bounce toward me across the rocks. To my surprise the line went taut. A gentle tug failed to dislodge the fly. My gaze wandered down the line, followed it, expecting to see the line lodged between two rocks. Instead the line disappeared, and I found myself staring into that baleful eye of the cat Puddy One-Eye. While my back was turned, Puddy had feasted on the salmon egg, swallowed it fly and all. Somewhere deep within that swarthy gullet was my beautiful golden prize. Attached to the strand of monofilament, Puddy One-Eye crouched there, the cat that had swallowed the canary-colored fly hook. I thought Puddy might cough up the lure like he might a hairball. Not a chance. No amount of gentle tugs could dislodge the hook. My initial tug must have set the hook somewhere in the bowels of that black cat. I had no choice but to take my jackknife, clip the line where it disappeared into the black maw, and loose the cat. Amid a hail of expletives and maledictions Puddy One-Eye slunk off, pregnant with my yellow fly.

That fall a spectacular fire destroyed all eight cabins of the riverbank bunkhouse. The fire broke out while the tenants were eating supper in the cookhouse, so fortunately no one was injured. The flames leaped against the autumn sky, scarred the night, illuminated the riverbank. The camp stood by helpless on the cookhouse lawn watching roof, walls collapse in sheets of sparks. We children stood with them, agog with excitement, mesmerized by the heat and destruction. By the time the Brewster pumper truck arrived, the structure was reduced to a hundred foot bed of embers that winked and flickered against the dark. Days later I probed the charred wreckage. Amid the scorched bricks, singed sinks, and heaps of charred debris I found the carcass of a small animal, cat-size. With a stick I probed the burnt rack of skeleton, sloughed the white flesh from the bones. Nowhere could I find a golden fly hook. The cat's nine lives were spent. Puddy One-Eye had crossed his own path one last time.

There were the Johnson family cats, too. Of those that passed through our cat fancies, three stayed on long enough to become part of the history of our house on the river. One female cat the soft color of fog like the Sandburg poem was Claudia's cat. Muffin she called her pet. (Had she been mine, I would have named her Gray Malkin.) Muffin had dainty white socks and two or three litters of kittens while she resided with us there on the river. The cat of legend, however, was Winnie.

The afternoon was hot as I walked up the county road above the Braker place. One minute I was alone, the next I was tripping over a scrawny kitten. The earth had opened and suddenly there was this ginger kitten, bob-tailed, all legs, meowing piteously. Obviously the kitten was a castaway, starving: no telling how long it had wandered the roadside (dumped there, no doubt, by someone too craven to sack the cat in a weighted bag and toss it off the bridge). The kitten would not be denied but claimed me that moment; it was not about to let me continue on without it. My new companion was determined to dance between my feet, and I could not walk. Once I was unable to dodge the cat and stepped on its head. With this considerable interference at my ankles, I continued up the road, making very little progress. Finally I had enough of this dance and scooped the little fellow up. I noticed dried blood inside one ear and was afraid I had injured the animal, stomped it too hard. (Some earlier misfortune apparently had caused the bloodshed.) I would carry the cat awhile, set it down to walk on its own. Then our dance would begin anew until I gave in to fear I would do the creature greater damage, carried it again. I named my cat dancing Winifred and took her home

The kitten's name did not stick long. Not only was the name too lofty for the tough little vagabond, but it was a misnomer: the cat was a "Fred," not a "Winnie." The sexing of kittens was not a skill of mine: initially I misread the kitten's posterior and diagnosed the terrain as female. Certain unfeminine behaviors the next few weeks led to a second inspection. This time there was no mistaking the male geography; a sex change had occurred. Regardless of the gender confusion, the kitten remained female in name. Winnie, we called him, his second name—that is until he proved tomcat enough to warrant a third.

I first thought the bob-tailed kitten to be something Manx, one of those cats with a nub for a tail. Winnie's tail, however, was too long to be termed a stub, too short to perform the swishing maneuver necessary for feline dignity. The tail rode the base of Winnie's spine like a ship's mast snapped by a high wind. Slide your hand along the appendage and you felt the bone underlayment twist into a pig's curlicue at the end as if something had kinked it.

This anomaly of tail proved to be an expression of Winnie's DNA. Somewhere in his chromosomal wardrobe lurked the twisted tail gene. The trait must have been dominant because it surfaced in a litter of cats, a bold statement that testified to their paternity. One of the kittens, (a ginger cat, also), we called Bobbus because his tail was a helixed afterthought, the bony substrata even more confused than his sire's. Another littermate displayed a spectacular manifestation of the kinky tail trait. In this case the kitten's tail rose perpendicular for half its length, took a hard turn left, then jutted off at a severe right angle. The unfortunate cat had to walk through life as if it were perpetually signaling a left hand turn. And though it may have been mean-spirited of us, we had little choice but to name the kitten "L" cat. What a cruel genetic prank for a father to pull on his offspring.

One Sunday morning Winnie played a trick on me, too, a foul act of tom-cat-foolery that earned him his third and final name. I was lying on the living room floor, the Sunday funnies spread before me. Intent on the latest installment of "Terry and the Pirates" and "The Phantom," I did not see the cat. Suddenly my face was wet. I looked up through dewy glasses to see a cat's ass and a pulsing, twisted tail. Oh, yuck! I had been cat sprayed! Winnie had reaffirmed his claim on me: I was his territory and had the dripping face to prove it. I avenged my cat spray baptismal by re-christening Winnie one last time. "Bathroom Going Winnie" (BGW) or "Bee Gee Dbyah" was his name thereafter.

From that moment on we were vigilant whenever BGW was about. If you were not careful, he would back up to you and let fly. For BGW foul was fair, and his persistence increased. "Watch out, he's backing up!" became a familiar alarm. You would look down to find BGW in reverse, sidling up to you. Then you had to act decisively. Before that tail began to pulsate, priming the pump, you reached down, grabbed his corkscrew, and redirected his equipment. The cat would retreat in a huff and bide his time, waiting for another victim to irrigate. Strange gratitude for the family who had opened their doors to an orphan.

One fall BGW disappeared without a trace. The next spring as I was exploring the riverbank below the packing shed, I stumbled upon the carcass of a ginger cat. The corpse had lain there throughout the winter but not long enough to fade the stain of dried blood from beneath that abbreviated, twisted tail.

Calico was third in our triad of cats. Her story I tell only for its shock value, for at each telling, the tale is certain to rattle the foundations of maternal instincts or sentiments. As cats go, Calico was ordinary. A female, like all calicos, her name derived from her piebald coat. But as a mother Calico was a marvel, an astonishment, and a horror. Hers is a story of a macabre maternity.

In a basket under the house one spring, Calico gave birth to a double digit family, a full baker's dozen, I believe. The basket bulged, seethed with tiny bodies. To gaze upon this caboodle of kittens brought to mind Wanda Ga'g's story *Millions of Cats*, made her tale of feline excess seem plausible. We visited the cellar often to marvel at the mass of fur churning against Calico's belly.

Two weeks passed. Mother and family seemed to be doing fine. The kittens grew. The curiosity of a basement full of kittens waned, and our visits down cellar decreased. One day I thought I would visit Calico and her brood to see if the kittens' eyes were open yet, if they had reached this milestone in feline development. On this occasion the sea of kittens seemed unusually calm; a strange torpor enveloped the basket. Naptime, I thought. I singled out a cute ginger head, reached in to stroke between its ears. No, its eyes were still closed. Calico raised her head warily. Gently, with my forefinger I stroked the sleeping head. To my surprise it rolled like a ball; the head rolled free and easy like a fur ball. In dismay I stroked a second, a gray one. It too flipped over. Under the perfectly formed ears were eyes, nose, and mouth: everything where it should be. Except there was no body. I sorted through the litter. Finally I found a complete kitten. I inventoried the basket and tallied seven kittens–and six bodiless heads. Calico had kept all her kittens in one basket and it had not worked out. In disgust I realized the fate of the bodies. In a most extreme act of population control, Calico the matron had turned Calico the cannibal. The stress of nursing that many mouths had drained her physically. To sustain the remaining seven, Calico had consumed their littermates' bodies: "Done," as Jude's son Father Time expressed in his murder/ suicide note, "Because we are too many."

I removed the six little heads and arranged them neatly in a coffee can. A sad sight they were in the bottom of the can: six miniature heads, twelve eyes that would never open, twelve eyes shut in permanent slumber. I buried the can somewhere in the orchard. Survived in their deaths were Bobbus and "L" Cat. At least the deceased were spared the indignities of a life in which great sport would be made of their tails.

And Animals

We tried our hand at other livestock on the river. The pear tree by the cookhouse miraculously fruited, not with partridges, but a brace of chickens, a hen and rooster. One night a ranch hand stealthily climbed the tree and snatched the sleeping pair from their roost high up in the branches. That was my launch into the poultry business. When the strawberry blonde hen I named Henny Penny yielded up the first egg, I became a confirmed capitalist. My friend Alan Johnson supplied me with a half dozen rag tag banties, and with this motley flock I became a chicken farmer. The egg business was hit and miss in its early stages. The way the dowdy little hens hid their eggs would have shamed the Easter bunny. The girls would rather set their eggs than yield them up. Regular searches of the chokecherry and snakeweed thicket next to the backyard cottonwood rarely turned up anything. When I did uncover a clutch of eggs, I was reluctant to market them as I didn't know how far along they were in the incubation cycle. No surer way to lose a customer than her crack an egg against the cake bowl and drop a bloody mess of fetal chick into the cake batter. And so for the time being I would relinquish the nest to the brooding hen and count on maternal instinct to swell my egg laying population.

Only when I built a ramshackle chicken coop just off the clothesline yard did egg production increase. Then I was able to collect eggs on a more regular basis. Even then egg production was sporadic, one week's harvest barely enough to fill one egg carton. Margaret Jean Crane was my only customer. She claimed the pint-sized eggs gave her baked goods a yellow hue.

In winter the little flock huddled around the one bare bulb I hung from the coop rafters, insufficient heat to keep the severe cold from seeping through the clapboard walls. Frostbite would blacken their combs and wattles. I mixed crushed eggshells with the hen scratch for a grit substitute as sand and gravel were buried and frozen beneath the snow. To match the temperature outside, winter egg production dropped to zero.

One spring I decided to diversify into row cropping and planted a strawberry patch. The chickens met this project with great enthusiasm, camped out in the rows, made quick work of the ripening berries, and scratched out the plants for good measure. The poultry business lost its bloom. I wrung a few necks and thinned some of the fleet of foot with the shotgun. The rest I gave away. All that remained of the Johnson chicken ranch was a manure-filled coop. Once again our eggs came from strangers, gathered weekly from the egg crates at Johnny's Market.

Baa-Baa

My farming horizons broadened further when I joined Brewster High's local chapter of the Future Farmers of America. My decision was a drastic one considering my sole motivation for becoming a future farmer was that membership offered all future farmers a two day reprieve from school so that the Vo-Ag boys might attend the week long Okanogan County Fair where we displayed varying degrees of ineptness in cattle judging and tractor driving. I myself garnished several fair ribbons and twenty plus dollars in prize money for a half dozen exhibits I hastily arranged from a cornucopia of fruit I gathered from the ranch. The money was perhaps the easiest I ever earned as all I had to do was shine a few plums and apples on my pant leg, pluck a plump cluster of grapes, and display this bounty from the field on paper plates, most of which sported red or blue ribbons after the judging.

What goes around, comes around, the saying goes, and it came around next spring when I discovered to pass the class, I had to choose and successfully complete a Vo-Ag project. Our instructor Mr. Killian told the class that the spring lambing was in progress on one of the local ranches and that a half dozen lambs ended up orphans. I was taken by the romantic vision of the good shepherd, put in my bid for one of the black sheep, and one afternoon after school Mr. Killian delivered Baa-Baa and Project Good Shepherd officially began.

Being a surrogate ewe for Baa-Baa was demanding work. The lamb consumed one bottle of milk after another and bleated for more, all the while waggling her long tail with glee. The empty chicken coop worked well as a temporary pen. As if she were a dog, the sheep followed me everywhere. I even took her to the hills to play hide and seek, would run off from her, hunker down in the rocks and wait to be found. After a few moments of desperate bleating and bounding through the brush, she would discover my hiding place, rush to me, and butt my crotch, hoping to coax forth a nipple.

The exclusive diet of milk gave the lamb the scours; her tail dripped with a foul, mustardy discharge. About the same time she caught a cold and then she oozed at both ends. This shepherd business was turning unpleasant—in truth, downright disgusting. Nor did it ever improve; one unpleasantness followed another.

It is customary for sheep men to dock their animals, lop their tails to a nub so the appendages would not wag about and soil the wool. I did not welcome this task (apparently neither did Mary of nursery rhyme lore, who allowed her charges to wander home with tails a' wagging behind them), but since it fell to the lot of a shepherd, I was determined to perform the surgery on my own animal. I did not have proper equipment for the procedure. A pruning shears would sever the tail. To cauterize the bleeding stub, I would use Dad's soldering iron. The only thing I lacked now was the courage to proceed. The bigger the sheep, I knew, the greater trauma the operation would cause. One day after school I plugged in the iron, gathered up the shears, and headed for the chicken coop.

I took my lamb to the back porch where the soldering iron smoked and clamped her head between my knees. With my left hand, I grabbed the protesting animal's tail and with a swift nip of the shears lopped off all but two inches. Tiny jets of blood sprayed from the wound. The lamb struggled to free itself, bleating horribly. It seemed to me there was far too much blood. Sensing the urgency of the situation and fighting back panic, I snatched up the smoldering iron and pressed it against the spurting wound. The iron sizzled and hissed. Scorched flesh, blood, wool cloyed my nostrils. The sheep fought my knees in pain and fear. Sear as I would, one or two stubborn vessels still streamed, would not staunch. Against the struggle of the lamb I applied the iron again and again. Finally the blackened iron shut the wounds. The spurting stopped. I released my lamb. The shoddy affair, akin to some seedy back alley operation, was, thank God, over. The next day when I presented the bottle, the lamb wiggled her stub as if nothing had happened.

Perhaps it would be appropriate at this point to comment on the intellect of a sheep. Now chickens, from my dealings with them, are known more for eggs and cacciatore than SAT scores, but compared to a sheep they are candidates for Mensa. Sheep, I discovered, were pretty much governed by their gut, and even then they could not decide whether to keep their food down or spew it up. There was no reasoning with the animal. Once she was weaned, the lamb had no more need of me; the bottle with the black nipple might as well have been a bomb. The sheep became a constant vexation. She gave over the bottle for the blossoms and buds of fruit trees and would strip the vegetation from any branch within reach. When I tried to catch, to stop her, she bolted away to the next tree and resumed her incorrigible nipping. Yield per acre around the house was sure to drop if I did not rein in my project. Besides, when spray season began, her voracious browsing would prove fatal. I would have to corral her.

Tethering the sheep was my next step. It proved to be a bad joke on me. I collared the lamb, secured one end of rope to her collar, the other to a tree stump on the lower lawn. I placed a bucket of water within her reach and went about my business. A half hour later plaintive bleating summoned me back. I found the water bucket upended and the sheep supine, its legs flailing in panic. I unknotted her and gave it another try. The results were the same: the sheep would be free or strangle itself. I freed her again, put aside my other business, and immediately began to construct a pen.

Not until I built the pen did that sheep give me a moment's rest. Even then it tried to escape a time or two, threaded its legs through the hogwire fencing and had to be extricated. A few minor adjustments secured the animal. From then on its only demands on my time and patience were the routine feedings of alfalfa pellets and daily waterings. The sheep was a hearty eater and in no time took on enough weight and size she could no longer outrun me. I sometimes released her to roam wider pastures. This I did only a time or two because she loved her new-found freedom and was reluctant to relinquish it. Then I would take a two-fisted purchase of her wooly back, drag the protesting sheep back to her pen, and lock her up.

Other young shepherds, curry combs in hand, spent hours cajoling their pets into soft lanoline sculptures. I, on the other hand, could foster no fondness for that sheep. From the onset of our relationship she was an annoyance: to me an insensate alimentary canal swaddled in wool. Had I the patience to wait for the fall sheep migrations, I would have ferried her across the river to join her wooly fellows—a reunion of dumb and dumber.

I sold my project to Bill Gebhardt. Come fair time, Baa-Baa was lamb chopped, cut and wrapped, in Bill and Marie's freezer, and I had fifty dollars in my pocket. Fifty dollars and a lambskin, stretched on a board and rock salted down out behind the woodshed, a reminder, each time I passed it, of the bad times that were.

George

Our neighbors the Whites bought a couple of cages and ventured into the chinchilla business, hoping to strike it rich in the fur trade. (Their fools gold dream went bust, as the delicate little creatures, which seemed to me a crazy hybrid of rabbit and squirrel, either succumbed to disease or sneezed themselves to death from the pumice-like ash they dusted in to rid themselves of mites. I do not believe they harvested a single pelt.) Not to be outdone, we Johnsons built a cage or two, stocked them with guinea pigs, and set out to learn the husbandry of these little animals. What we did learn about them was: they occasionally bit, cranked out bean-shaped manure pellets, squeaked loudly when they were hungry, made a soft chirring noise when they were contented or angry, or frightened or horny, copulated quickly and often, and sometimes killed their babies. Though we must have tended nearly a dozen of these agreeable little fellows during our experience with them, and perhaps named them all, only one deserves a mention in the annals of our family's history on the river.

A short-haired guinea, George was the size of a large russet baked potato, Irish red in color. George was remarkable in that he was a free range guinea pig most of his life. Though I forget the particulars, somehow George escaped to the chokecherry thicket behind the cottonwood tree (where the chickens hid their eggs) and had the run of the place. Though difficult to catch, he was never hard to find, so we acknowledged his freedom and let him roam at will. George occasionally ventured beyond the cover of the thicket to browse in the orchard, but he never strayed far from safety. During the summer the orchards were routinely sprayed with insecticide. We feared for George's safety then, concerned he might ingest a lethal amount of spray residue in his grazings. Thus would begin the great guinea pig round-up.

I doubt we would have been able to catch George had it not been for Tiny. The guinea pig was wily and swift, squirted through the grass like a greased snake. No sooner would the chase begin than he would dart into the thicket. He was safe from us there, so we would enlist Tiny to root him out. Show Tiny George's run, point to the worn trace, and with a "Go get 'em, Tiny," he would dive into the thicket. There would be a thrashing and crashing about in the brush and George would spurt out. Like beaters on safari we would insert our forces between George and his thicket and let Tiny complete the capture. To this day I marvel at my dog's gentleness, his understanding that we wanted–expected–George to be restrained but not harmed. Once George was in the open, Tiny quickly pinned him gently beneath his front paws, held him down in the grass until one of us removed the squirming, chirring spud to the safety of his cage. For two or three weeks George would remain penned, long enough for the residual toxins to dissipate, and then we would release him to his thicket again.

For two or three summers this was our routine with George (winters we kept him penned safe and warm in the house). You would have thought George might have fallen prey to some predator. Cats, even a big tom, I doubt would have tackled the guinea pig, for he weighed nearly three pounds. But to a stray dog or coyote, George would have been a tender feast.

Ironically, George's fate did not come from some marauder in the night, nor was he, like the chinchillas, carried off by some disease. I am aware, now that I write this history, how hard I was on the animals of the place, and George is testimony to this fact.

Sometimes we kept George beneath an upturned crate while awaiting the last spray to wane. We would find some grassy area beyond the spray drift and pen George there. Periodically throughout the day we would scoot the box and George to new pasture. One day the family had an outing planned. Before I climbed in the car, I remembered George and his crate had not been relocated for some time. Hurriedly, I ran to the crate, scooted it. We used a large stone to weight the crate. I replaced it and returned to the car.

Later, after our return, I went to check on George. I thumped the crate, which usually set him a' chirring. Silence. I discovered why when I lifted the crate. In my haste to slide the box, I had pinned George's head, squashed it beneath the rim of the crate. The rock I thumped down on the crate was the *coup-de-grace*, George's a death, of sorts, by stoning.

Petpourri

Tim coveted an exotic monkey, a pigmy primate the size, according to the black and white photo in the *Boys' Life* advertisement, that could nestle in the bowl of a teacup. The half-pint primate was a promotion to sell a brand of salve purported to have a number of health-giving properties: hawk so many cases of the balm and you got a cupful of monkey for your services. Tim peddled the stuff, jumped through numerous other hoops as well, but it was never quite enough. Tim's cup came up empty each time. In the end, the fine print got the best of brother Tim, and his monkey business ended in disappointment.

It was just as well. Cranes had their own monkey, not a miniature, but a spider monkey that required a cage for confinement, not a teacup. One day Margaret Jean was entertaining her friend

Lorraine Cox, took her around to the monkey's cage to show off their pet. No sooner had the introduction taken place than the monkey decided to do a little monkey business of his own, lifted his tail, grabbed a hefty handful of warm excrement and flung it at Lorraine. Though spackled and surprised, all Lorraine's decorum would allow was, "My! They're messy little fellows, aren't they!" Somehow the monkey escaped to the out-of-doors and could not be caught. It slept nights in the three fir trees at the entrance to our driveway. I remember being startled to look up and find a monkey walking the power lead to our house like it was a tightrope. For a moment I thought the circus had come to town. During a stretch of cold weather the monkey caught pneumonia and died. That was just as well, too.

After the monkey shuffled off, Francis replaced him with a series of raccoons. These arrived at the ranch as pups. Cranes then raised them to burley adults, at which time they reverted to the wild and left the ranch to seek their respective fortunes on the riverbank or up the canyon.

Do not be deceived by their cute ears and quaint mask: a raccoon by nature is a varmint. Beneath those ears and mask is a mouth of vicious teeth honed by a nasty disposition. As long as one is about, no good can come of it. Toby, Cranes' first 'coon, somehow got into our house. The rascal ravaged a roll of toilet paper, shredded and strewed it all over the house, moved on to Claudia's fishbowl, downed a couple of occupants before we could evict it. Nothing was safe from this masked villain. I was working on a modeling project on the back porch, reached for my tube of Duco Cement and came away with a handful of glue—the 'coon had chomped the tube into a gluey mess. You never knew what mischief it would be up to next—until a snorting and snuffling interrupted your river-bank reverie, and you turned to find a striped head buried up to the ears in your can of fish worms. Then you knew.

Another 'coon had a fascination for bedsheets drying on the clothesline, would latch onto their flapping sails, and swing there until they ripped. One night as I wandered home by the junipers next to the little lawn, the same critter launched himself with a "woof" onto my shoe tops. I nearly wet myself in fright. Ever after I made sure to give the junipers a wide berth whenever I passed them in the dark.

Cranes' third raccoon was every bit the scoundrel of his predecessors. He was the scourge of camp. Leave your pet food unattended and chances were your pets would come up lean while the 'coon grew fatter. A fat turkey set out to thaw lost weight too. When its owner went to check the progress, he found a bloodied, mangled carcass. It was as though the bird had been assaulted by a meat saw. Thawed or frozen, little matter: the 'coon was unquestionably a breast man.

Wherever there was food, this masked rogue was always first at the picnic. It was in this way Fred Faircloth, one of the regular crew fell afoul of it. Fred was a young fellow who saw to his work through thick, dust-coated glasses. His face was an eruption of pimples, which he tried to hide beneath the underbrush of sideburns and facial hair. As yet, Fred was not man enough to set a beard, and except for random patches of linty fuzz, his blemishes had little cover.

Fred and his newlywed wife Betty rented a place in town. From what I knew of Betty her main passions seemed to be soap operas and the copious amounts of boxed candy she ate to sustain herself during the afternoon binges of electronic trauma. I had the sense Fred and his unborn child (I suspect Betty's dual status of pregnant and newlywed had a cause and effect explanation) were not among her passions and doubt Betty knew their marriage had the makings of a soap opera itself.

One morning in late spring Fred drove to work, parked his car next to the cookhouse, and because the days had been warm, left his window down for ventilation. At noon we knocked off for lunch. Fred's car was on my way home, so we walked to lunch together. I was glad I did, otherwise I might have missed the fun because when Fred came to his car, he found Cranes' 'coon had knocked off a little early for lunch—Fred's, that is. There on the front seat, passenger side, with a brown paper sack spread before him, squatted the raccoon. It had appropriated half a sandwich and was making short work of it. Five o'clock and supper were a long way off, so Fred grabbed the door handle and swung the door open to salvage what was left of his lunch. This action brought immediate displeasure from the thief. It hissed and snarled, rolled its upper lip nearly to the mask, showed razor teeth that dripped lunchmeat and bread. Now unless your primary caregiver is close at hand and you know your blood type, cornering a raccoon is an unwise thing to do. Fred made a couple more attempts to assert himself, but they were half-hearted. The stand-off continued, Fred circling the car, all the while pounding on the windows and doors, each thump punctuated by a snarling from within and considerable prime ranch hand language from without. The 'coon finished the second half of the sandwich and rifled through the sack for dessert, which I think was a twin pack of Twinkies. Then it leisurely performed some post-meal hygiene, tidily licked its paws and apron. Watching Fred's every move, the 'coon shuffled to the window, climbed out, dropped to the ground, and giving Fred a parting growl (though it may have been a belch), it ambled off toward Crane's lawn. I had to hustle home, nearly missed my lunch, but the show had been worth it.

Fred was in a foul mood the rest of the day. Of course, I took every opportunity to explain the exact cause of Fred's spleen to the entire crew. That did little to smooth things over. As Fred and his stomach grumbled their way through the afternoon, I could not help but think of Betty in town, knocking back the chocolates, seduced by the flickering glow of *The Days of Our Lives*.

And Then There Were None

The magpie chicks came from somewhere down Dougherty Canyon. For a spring diversion Don and Larry Humborg plundered a magpie nest, a twisted jumble of sticks, the woof and warp of which entwined the branches of a serviceberry bush. They came away with five unkempt fledglings mostly all down and beak. And that's how we came by the five magpies.

Unlike the young of songbirds, which require a special diet and nonstop parental nurture, rendering it nearly impossible for human hands to tend them, magpies were a cinch to raise. Whenever you approached the boxful of chicks, you were greeted by five gaping mouths yammering for food. No pablum-filled eyedroppers or pried open beaks for these black and white chuckleheads. Bread crusts, leftover pancakes, hen scratch, no sooner did a morsel touch a tongue than it was gulped down gullet. While they ate, they closed their eyes, gobbled in blind trust whatever was thrust in their mouths. This blind greed proved the downfall of one of the chicks. Little sister Lisa dispatched that one with a chunk of asparagus stalk, which she shoved down its clamoring throat. The chick choked to death on the offering. Then there were four.

As the weeks passed, the remaining chicks fledged out and learned to fly. In spite of their new independence, their insatiable appetites kept them around the place, continuing to squawk and cackle for food. At night the magpies roosted in the cottonwood or an adjacent apple tree. First thing in the morning whenever one of us appeared, they would descend upon us like pigeons, mill about, beaks agape, shrieking for a handout. One morning I discovered if I shoved the wooden gun cleaning rod Dad made for his shotgun through the hole in the screen of my bedroom window, the four birds would flock en masse, land there and yammer for food. It was great fun to see them appear from nowhere at the sight of the waggling rod. They would alight and jostle each other, jockeying for position next to the screen, each wanting to be first in line for a handout. A quick twist of the wrist and they would tumble off, flap about the window, settle again, and resume their fussing. After a few minutes of bird baiting, I would retract their perch and go outside to feed the black and white clowns. This was my routine for a week or two that summer of the magpies.

One day one of the four flew up to investigate the transformer on the telephone pole set at the end of the lower lawn and was electrocuted for its curiosity. And then there were three. Whenever a breeze came up, the deceased's feathers would lift and fall.

A sibling noticed the flapping feathers, flew up to check them out. And then there were two.

I'm not sure what happened to the penultimate magpie. Perhaps he fell victim to a cat. Perhaps one of his fellows, a lady friend, lured him into the wild. We preferred to think he left for love, not as cat food. And then there was one.

Beeoh we called the sole magpie, the only bird of the five who survived long enough to warrant a name. I don't know how he came by Beeoh (the name may have come from a distinctive cry he made; magpies are mimickers, can parrot the calls of other birds—or humans, which was our hope). Though Beeoh was an able enough flier, something was wrong with his landing gear. From time to time it would collapse, tumble him. Thus, when he was earthbound, he walked with a stumble. Magpies, like all corvids, are scavengers. We believe Beeoh, while flensing Baa-Baa's curing sheepskin, may have accidentally ingested rock salt, causing nerve damage to his undercarriage. Might have been the case. As I've noted, magpies will eat anything.

That's why one afternoon while I was preparing to move water lines, I fed him raisins. For some reason Beeoh always showed up when I laced my tennis shoes. He would flap down on the back porch and wobble over to peck at my laces. This afternoon I was snacking on a handful of raisins and thought I'd toss one on the lawn to distract the pesky bird. Immediately Beeoh wobbled in pursuit, found the raisin and plucked it up. Imagine my surprise when he didn't eat it on the spot. Instead, Beeoh hobbled off to a patch of bare ground, found a hole, and dropped in the raisin. I tossed another. Beeoh scooped this up as well, returned to the hole, and dropped in the second. I threw a half dozen more, each of which Beeoh deposited in the hole as before. I ate the rest myself, laced up my shoes, and was about to head out for my shift, but the antics of the silly bird stopped me. When he realized that was the last of the raisins, he returned to the hole to retrieve his stash. Here I am reminded of the Twain story about a bluejay (a magpie's corvid cousin) that performed the same maneuver, though with acorns, dropping them through a knothole in the roof of a shack, unaware he was attempting to fill an entire house with nuts. Beeoh thrust his beak into the hole until he nearly stuck his head but couldn't retrieve a single raisin. He knew they were down there somewhere, would put his eye to the hole to see where they went. When his beak failed him again and again, his magpie temper flared. I left Beeoh circling the hole, squawking at it, scratching at the lip, pausing to peer into its depths for its plunder. Beeoh fussed and fumed about the hole, and again I hear Twain's words, "I never saw a jay carry on so."

The magpies were great pets, entertained us for hours, always good for a laugh. Beeoh lasted until dove season. Though he could hardly have been mistaken for a dove, he was probably downed for target practice by some trigger-happy hunter. And then there were none.

There were other animal stories, too: the weasel Kevin found trapped in a drain hole (he rescued the little fellow and as thanks, received a painful bite on the thumb). One summer day when the river was in flood, I saw an animal midstream, swimming frantically for shore. Some poor dog, I thought, and fully expected the struggling animal to disappear beneath the surface any minute. But the head kept coming, barely above the swirling surface, resolute, paddling steadily shoreward. At last the animal reached the eddying backwater. I knew then it would survive, reach the safety of the bank. I felt like cheering and ran down the bank to offer what help or encouragement I could.

What I found needed no help from me whatsoever. Instead of some hapless stray shaking by the willows, I found a badger. The animal lay where it had come ashore, too spent to pull itself from the water. The badger's head rested on the mud; which of us was more surprised it's hard to say. Immediately I sensed my presence was unwanted. In fact, if the badger had not been exhausted, I believe it would have chased me back the way I had come. I was clearly violating its personal space. The animal seethed, hissed, seemed to steam at my intrusion.

A badger is a solitary animal; the only difference between a badger and its fiendish larger cousin the wolverine is the latter goes through life looking for trouble, while a badger will not tolerate any. Both are exceptionally well-equipped to keep trouble at bay. Whatever the badger's affairs, I knew better than to meddle in them.

A badger came to camp one other time I remember. The story became a camp legend and was a favorite of Dad's. One fall during harvest three drunk Indians drove into camp. They were looking for work. Their condition, of course, did not lend itself to employment. Not the least bit rebuffed, one of the three asked if anyone wanted to buy a badger. Such a bizarre request was sure to pique the curiosity of any bystander. Three drunk Indians was novelty enough, and when it was discovered they were badger salesmen, several onlookers gathered. Someone half-jokingly asked to see the wares. The salesman walked to the rear of the old heap they had arrived in and opened the trunk. There, to the amazement of the audience, snarling and hissing at the attention, crouched a full grown badger. One of the crowd asked the Indian how he had caught the animal. "Like this," he replied, and with amazing swiftness for a drunk, the Indian feinted deftly at the badger's head with his left hand. The badger lunged at the hand and when it did, its captor grabbed a hind leg and snatched the enraged beast from the trunk. The salesman displayed his wares at arm's length, slowly swung the furious badger back and forth, obviously pleased to be center stage. His supporting actor was not. The Indian was soon upstaged. Whether it was the alcohol, the weight of the badger, or delivery of his sales pitch, each swing of the arm brought the badger closer to his captor's leg. Suddenly, as it swung by, the badger lunged and latched onto the Indian's calf. Next ensued a frantic dance and tug-of-war to dislodge the badger, who invested all its pent-up fury into its grip. Several tugs failed to detach the badger. Finally the Indian gave a desperate tug. With a rending of levis and flesh, he freed himself from the champing jaws. And again the badger swung at arm's length, this time smacking its lips as if it had savored a fine caviar. With a grunt of pain, Dances

With Badger flung the avenger into the trunk, slammed shut the lid, and their trunk again full of badger, the three drunks drove off, leaving a stunned audience behind in a cloud of harvest dust.

I was not among that audience, only knew the story through Dad. And whenever badgers were the topic, Dad would relate the tale of the three drunk Indians and their passenger. The highlight of the narrative for Dad—and the listener—was the part where the badger smacked its lips. "Smeck, smeck, smeck," Dad would mimic and laugh, "Smeck, smeck, smeck."

The Ol' Swimming Hole

August. Since the Fourth of July the river has ceded us the upper bank and the Old Dead Tree, inching daily closer to its bed. As it creeps downhill, the river leaves behind a thick skin of silt, sloughs it off, coating all it touches with a murky sludge. River musk bakes in the sun, pungent with oil of dead squawfish and carp. Snakeweed and willow, cottonwood and wildrose crud encased.

A red wing grasshopper hovers on air. Its staccato pyrotechnics, like an exploding chain of lady fingers, divert us. Instantly we seek it out, this most exotic of riverbank grasshoppers. Asparagus fronds in hand, we search the bank to spy where it rests, this shard of coal, hoping to snare it beneath the ferny bush, capture it and unfurl its flashy red wings like an oriental fan.

The river runs clear now, clear and cold. From vantage points on the bunkhouse porches or the bank by the packing shed, we observe the carp and suckers foraging the river bottom. From the green depths they reveal themselves, turn their flanks to the sun, and signal us like mirrors. We fish for them. They spurn our bait. We try to snag them. They avoid our hooks. Their presence excites us.

On the bank beneath The Old Dead Tree the river slips away, the worrisome current subsides, no longer a threat to snatch at a swimmer, pull him under. It is safe to swim. And to escape the August heat, that is what we want to do.

Among a pile of boards behind the tractor barn we find a plank. We add to it a fifty gallon drum from the junk heap beside the shop. Both we take to the bank below The Old Dead Tree. The plank is rough hewn, thick, ten or twelve feet long; there is no spring to it. We position the board on the lip of the bank, hold it in place with the drum, which we weight with rocks, sand, and water. Either side for support, like stilts, we nail two orchard props. From this vista, our diving board, we can fling ourselves into the depths of the river eight feet below.

In the August swelter the swimming hole beckons. No dawdling over our chores now. Rush through the work and down the bank we run. Beneath the board, a'glint with alluvia, the river crawls by cold. Run down the plank. Launch yourself, arms and legs windmilling into space. Then you plunge into May and the current tugs you. Surface, and flail against the tug before the bank leaves you behind. Scramble up the sandy path to drip and shiver until the sun bakes you dry. Then down the board and into space again.

That was our routine those summer days in August: frolic in the river from nine till noon. Out for lunch. Wait the cautionary hour to ward off the cramps. Then back to the swimming hole the rest of the afternoon. An occasional sultry evening we would launch ourselves into an August sunset, swim until dusk.

Sometimes on a hot afternoon Francis and Margaret Jean would saunter down the path and join us for a swim. Francis was a strong swimmer and with envy I watched him swim frogman style underwater against the current, his untanned body gleaming like a carp's belly beneath the surface. Others joined us, too, camp kids: the Shenyer boys, Mike and Larry, would trudge down the bank. They were non-swimmers and looked like stick figures in their over-sized life jackets. When they struck the water, their jackets buoyed up around their curly heads like kapok sausages, obscuring their view of the bank. We had to yell to keep them and their skinny arms from striking out for the opposite shore.

Even dogs joined in the swim. Dale Piggot's golden retrievers, Dusty and Goldie, enjoyed the swimming hole as much as we.

They were as comfortable in the water as they were in the hills, running Bud Priest's Herefords through barbed wire fences. Anything we flung in the water they would retrieve—even us. A favorite game was to stand on the tip of the plank and fling a rubber thong as far into the river as our arms could throw. Just before the dogs reached the thong, its owner leaped from the board, and as the dogs swam by, grabbed the closest tail and let himself be dog towed to shore. The retrievers had feet like paddles, and I'm sure each could have towed a small boat.

Days passed. The water receded. The big bellied river ran svelte again, nearly snug in its bed. The diving board now projected high and dry over sand and river cobbles and was abandoned. Though our days of running the plank were over, no matter—a reunion was imminent: west, downriver, first you saw the ripples break, heard the rush of current. A day or two later you awoke to find that during the night the river had delivered up the island. The same tumbled boulders split the rush of current, glistened dark and clean in the morning sun. To us these rocks of ages were a homecoming of memory, an overture to new adventures. In a week or two painstakingly we would wade the riffles across the spine of the island to its head, our tennis shoes betraying our balance every cautious step of the way. There we would reacquaint ourselves with each boulder, explore each crevice for treasures newly deposited. Then along the margins and shallows—the deep pool in the island's lee. Coffee cans and sticks in hand we probe the river cobbles for bullheads, which, as if they had burst, dart off in explosions of sand. Overturn a stone and find the first crawdad of the season, as ageless as a trilobite, darting hardfast in reverse, seeking refuge among the slimy cobbles, claws cocked and ready. The island: so old, so familiar. Our island: so new, so wondrous.

One day I awoke to find the hue of summer gone from the river. Apples, dappled, the size of grapefruit, swung heavy from the gravenstein. During the night the earth seemed to have slipped a notch forward. There appeared to be more shade, the shadows darker, outlines starker. In the afternoon a benign, gentler sun addressed the riverbank. The day seemed locked between closure and advent. Time put on pause. Even the fine dust of the place hung golden in the air. Change, I knew, was at hand. Soon the ranch on the riverbank would explode with the noise and frenzy of harvest. Downriver soon a cloud of dust would rise from the opposite bank, marking the plodding exodus of a thousand sheep from the Methow highlands. Soon one night, from the island in the river, a campfire would blaze from out the dark, its cheery glow dance and flicker across black waters. And soon the yellow bus would grind to a stop, open its doors, cart us off to another school year. Soon now. Any day.

POSTSCRIPT

Now he knew what grief was. It was the memory
of time past, of time in its poignant and irrevocable
pastness. It was a man's memory of being a child after it
was impossible any longer to be a child.

Johnny Shawnessy
Raintree County

In fall I had come to the riverbank. Fall ten years later I left it. That year for graduation, I was given a suitcase, a gift practical enough, but to me, recent alumnus of Brewster High, class of '62, the luggage represented a separation. Thus began a time of confusion and rebellion that lasted three, maybe four years. I could not put a name to it then. But those years I was an angry young man. It was as if I were in a rowboat cast loose from its moorings, set adrift, only one oar sound, the other snapped in half, broken and useless. Borne by the current I rowed in lazy circles, the riverbank receding with each revolution, the white ranch house ever smaller. Then finally I was swept around the bend of the river and all was gone. My wife explains my fitful passage from boyhood, the familiar to the unknown, as a period of grief. Perhaps she is right. There was no space in that suitcase for anything but the future, and with my suitcase bulging with the unknown, I turned my back on a magical childhood and the river.

Some forty years later I return to the sage uplands, and where we clambered among the rocks and greasewood, I find Chief Joseph's Table and Crevasse Rock, still massive, lichen-covered, immutable. But once, where the sagebrush flats stretched before them to the brow of the hill above the river, from their base, rows of fruit trees line the earth. The vista from which a man watched a young hunter lift a limp cottontail from the greasewood covert below, hold his first kill aloft in triumph, now presents row upon row of mature apple trees. I wondered at the man's thoughts, the father, the outdoorsman, sharing this rite of passage with the son. Thoughts of pride? Perhaps nostalgia? His first kill? I stand where the man stood and in subsequent years the son, watching a frenzied little dog cast for game across the brushy flats where fruit trees now shadow the earth.

I hike east, toward Pond Rock, passing some of the way through new orchard. I cross no fences this time. Only the ravine is familiar, its banks ever pocked by the holes of nesting bank swallows. Beyond the ravine here too the landscape has changed. The sagelands where Pond Rock seemed to float like an ark now sprouted orchard south and east. A horse corral west of the rock encloses three tenants. A poplar-lined drive leads to Barclay Crane's massive house, which now competes with the view of Billygoat Mountain, the Sawtooths, and the Methow Valley.

Barclay's citadel rises from the brow of the westward hill, towers above the sagebrush like Riatta on the movie set of **Giant.** A dozen feet from Pond Rock, lying among clumps of tousled bunch grass I find something even more incongruous. A baseball. I pick it up, turn the ball in my hand. The stitching has lifted. The hide is scuffed and weathered, now textured like a tennis ball. How it came to rest here I have no idea. A baseball seizes the hearts of men and again they become boys. I stand in the shadow *of Pond Rock, twist the weathered sphere in my hand, toss it gently upwards, catch it as it falls. In that gesture the years seem to spin away, revealing a boy who played here, climbed these very rocks, gazed into the pools, waters which now reflect a stranger's face. I tuck the ball away in my camera case, turn to the west, and begin the trek back.*

This day a stiff breeze lashes a gray chop against the protesting current. Reeds and cattails choke the old driveway, bend and clatter in the wind. My gaze lifts across the water, far to the opposite bank where the sheep came each fall. I search for a landmark, a sign for direction. Nothing signifies. Somewhere upriver, frightened by the intruder, geese take flight in anger. Eastward, toward their protesting cries, I walk a strange margin beside a strange lake, a stranger here myself, to myself.

A gust of wind keens against me. A good day to launch a kite. What message would I send spinning along the bellying string, twisting upwards? No message. A question, perhaps. To what height must I go to bring it all back again? How high to see beneath the wind-raked water an island where boys cluster around a crackling fire, their faces aglow with excitement, adventure? Higher still? A boy, clasping schoolbooks, calls a name and up the dusty drive to greet him sideways lopes a little lion of a dog. A gleeful reunion: as if it were the first, as it would be the last. And perhaps if I were to perch on high, against the flutter of the kite, hover with it on the wind, I could see a fleck of red far across the water on the distant bank below the big rock. A steelhead fisherman in a red Mackinaw, casting, retrieving, casting again. A kind and gentle man contending with that great river for just one more fish.

The Riverbank

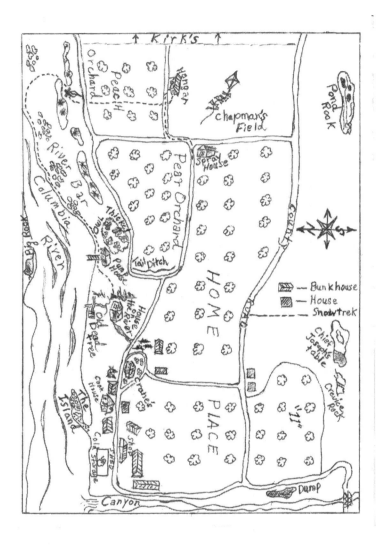

Made in the USA
Charleston, SC
14 June 2016